BASICS

CONSTRUCTION
SCHEDULING

\\ BERT BIELEFELD

BASICS

CONSTRUCTION SCHEDULING

BIRKHÄUSER
BASEL·BOSTON·BERLIN

CONTENTS

FOREWORD

Coordinating the planning and construction process is a complex task, which involves a great deal of responsibility, especially in larger building projects. Due both to the increasing interconnection between components and to the specialization of contractors, a large number of participants and their work must be organized. Scheduling is the most important means by which project planners control the entire process. It forms the basis of the contractual deadlines given to the participating construction companies, and is also a tool that is used actively to respond to unforeseen happenings and disruptions during the planning and construction process.

Due to their lack of experience, university graduates and entry-level professionals embarking on their initial projects are often unsure of how to manage the participants in the planning and construction process. Typical questions are: What work must be coordinated? What is the sequence of work steps? And how long do these steps last? *Basics Construction Scheduling* is directed at students and entry-level professionals at this early stage of the game. In a step-by-step, practical way, it shows how a schedule is created, how it represents the planning and construction process, and how it can be used as a tool in the real world.

Bert Bielefeld, Editor

INTRODUCTION

The translation of an initial idea into a completed building is a lengthy and extremely complex undertaking. The large number of people involved—construction contractors, planners and owner-builders—make it necessary to coordinate all the different contributions to the process closely.

Architects and project planners represent the owner in technical matters and must work to ensure that the entire process runs as smoothly as possible. Looking after the owner's interests, they coordinate all the participants in the planning process and monitor the contractors on the construction site. Larger projects often entail twenty to thirty participants or more in the planning and construction processes, which results in complex links and interdependencies. The various participants are often unable to understand or judge how their specific work is linked to the project workflows as a whole. As a result, architects have a special coordinating responsibility since their planning encompasses the entire range of specialized tasks involved in a project, and they are therefore the only participants in the process who have the "big picture."

Scheduling is a tool that is used in all stages of this process. The present book explains its foundations and applications, addressing all forms and depths of representation and providing practical information on typical processes. Its goal is to give students a quick, real-world introduction to the material. Yet coordination work is not over once a schedule has been created. It is a work process that must be constantly updated and made more precise. A good deal of preliminary consideration and refinement of detail is required in order to specify the phases into which work on a site is ultimately organized. The following chapters describe which participants and steps need to be taken into account when creating a schedule.

CREATING A SCHEDULE

SCHEDULE ELEMENTS

To begin with, a description of a few key terms and the various elements of a schedule is in order.

Period and deadline

Planners distinguish between a deadline and a time period. The word <u>deadline</u> describes a specific point in time, such as the day on which part of a project must be completed, while a <u>period</u> is a span of time (e.g. completion of a job within fourteen days).

Tasks

<u>Tasks</u> are the very foundation of the schedule and refer to self-contained work units (e.g. tiling the ground floor). If several tasks are combined (e.g. tiling and plastering), the result is a <u>summary task</u> › Chapter Creating a schedule, The structure of the project schedule

Planning the duration and sequence of tasks

<u>Task duration</u> is the time needed to complete a task. It is a factor of production quantity and productivity. › Chapter Creating a schedule, Planning task duration

The calculation of duration is referred to as <u>duration planning</u>. Establishing the dependencies between activities is referred to as <u>sequence planning</u>. Taken together, duration and sequence planning form the basis of <u>construction scheduling</u>. › Fig. 1

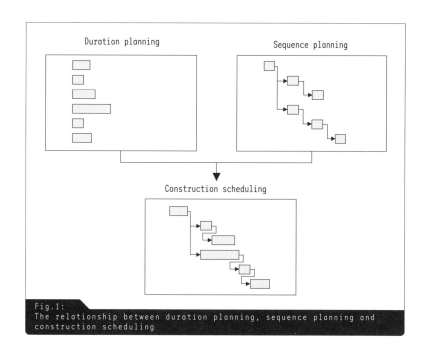

Fig.1:
The relationship between duration planning, sequence planning and construction scheduling

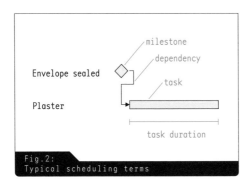

Fig.2:
Typical scheduling terms

Construction
methods and
resources

Construction method refers to the technical procedure for carrying out a task.

The equipment and labor necessary to perform a task are called resources. While preparing for a building project, construction companies plan their resources in order to calculate costs precisely and define construction methods. The result serves as the foundation for their bid. While calculating resources has only limited significance for the architect doing the scheduling, smooth workflow requires a realistic assessment of task durations, for which resource planning provides a foundation. › Chapter Creating a schedule, Depth of representation

Milestones

A milestone is a task without a duration. It is a special event entered separately into the schedule. Typical scheduling milestones include the start of construction, completion of the building structure, sealing the building envelope, final inspection and putting the building into operation. › Fig. 2

Dependencies
between tasks

In most cases, tasks are not isolated items on the schedule but are integrated into a web of dependencies with other tasks. There can be several reasons for this. The normal case is a sequential dependency: task B can

\\ Example:
In any construction process there may be many ways to achieve the desired results. For instance, a reinforced concrete ceiling may be built of prefabricated elements or cast on site. Wall tiles can be laid in a thin bed on plaster or in a thick bed on a rough wall.

only begin once task A is finished (e.g. ground-floor walls → ground-floor ceiling → upper-floor walls).

That said, some tasks can only be performed jointly in a parallel process (e.g. setting up scaffolding floor by floor as the structure of a multistory building goes up). Often these process dependencies can be broken down into sequential dependencies by using a higher level of detail.

By contrast, it is often impossible for finishing contractors to work in parallel during a number of construction phases (e.g. screed and plastering work). In this case we speak of one task <u>interfering</u> with another. This is why it is essential for planners to examine mutual dependencies between specialized tasks and, if necessary, to divide the project into optimal construction phases. › Chapter **Creating a schedule, Planning task sequence** and Chapter **Workflows in the planning and construction process**

Types of relationships

›

Various types of relationships play an important role in the graphic representation of dependencies between two tasks. Construction scheduling distinguishes between four types: › Fig. 3

_ <u>Finish-to-start</u>: Task B can only begin after task A is finished. This is the most common type of relationship and may apply to activities such as the construction of interior walls (A) and interior plastering (B).
_ <u>Finish-to-finish</u>: Task A and task B must be completed by the same time. This type of relationship exists when tasks A and B provide the foundation for an additional task. Examples are installing windows (A) and sealing the roof (B), which create the airtight building envelope necessary for interior work.
_ <u>Start-to-finish</u>: Task B must end when task A begins. In this type of relationship, one task can be scheduled at the latest possible point in time before it interferes with another task.

\\ Note:
If sequential dependencies are not examined in detail during scheduling work, the result can often be disruptions and delays in the construction process. If, for instance, a disabled-accessible, steel-framed door needs to be installed, the required electrical outlets must be installed before plastering is done. Overlooking such dependencies may result in further work being required on finished surfaces.

\\ Tip:
The most popular construction scheduling programs support the types of relationships described above. As a rule, they assign each task its own number, which can be used to denote dependencies. For example, if a task needs to begin after task no. 5, the previous task is marked 5FTS, where FTS stands for a finish-to-start relationship.

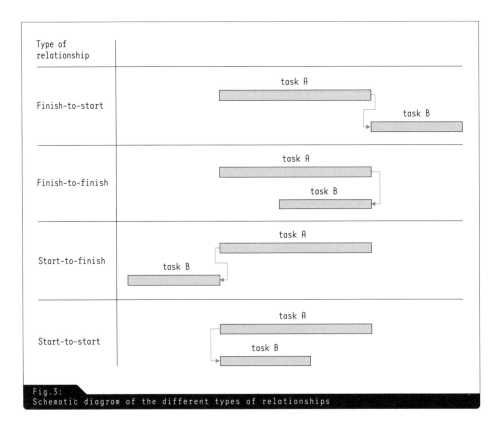

Type of relationship	
Finish-to-start	task A task B
Finish-to-finish	task A task B
Start-to-finish	task A task B
Start-to-start	task A task B

Fig.3:
Schematic diagram of the different types of relationships

_ Start-to-start: Task A and task B must start at the same time. This makes sense if the work can be performed in parallel—if, for instance, workers from one trade can use a crane that is operated by another contractor to deliver large building elements.

FORMS OF REPRESENTATION

There are different ways to represent a schedule graphically. The following forms of representation are used to communicate schedule contents in a clear and useful manner, depending on the goal and purpose of the schedule: › Fig. 4

_ Bar chart
_ Line diagram
_ Network diagram
_ Deadline list

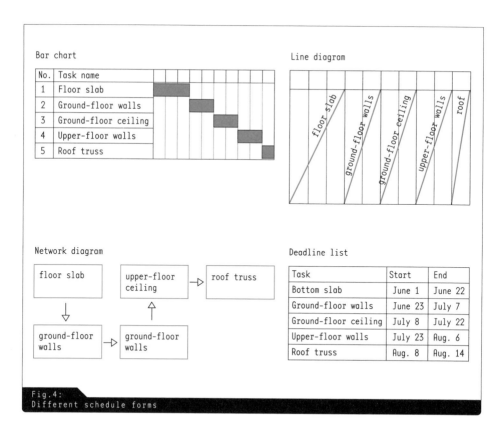

Fig.4:
Different schedule forms

In building construction, schedules are normally shown as <u>bar charts</u>, also called <u>Gantt diagrams</u>. Time is charted along the horizontal axis, and the various tasks are listed along the vertical axis. The duration of each task is recorded as a horizontal bar along the corresponding time axis. › Fig. 5

The time axis can be divided into months, weeks and days, depending on project scope and the required degree of detail. In addition to graphically representing activities, this form of schedule commonly incorporates related information in the left-hand column to facilitate easy reading (e.g. task description, starting date, completion date, duration and, if necessary, dependencies with other tasks). Dependencies are often shown graphically as arrows between different bars.

The basic structure of a <u>line diagram</u> differs from that of a bar chart in that the units executed are shown on the second axis next to the time-line. The tasks are depicted by lines in the coordinate system. The following types of line diagrams are commonly used in the construction industry:

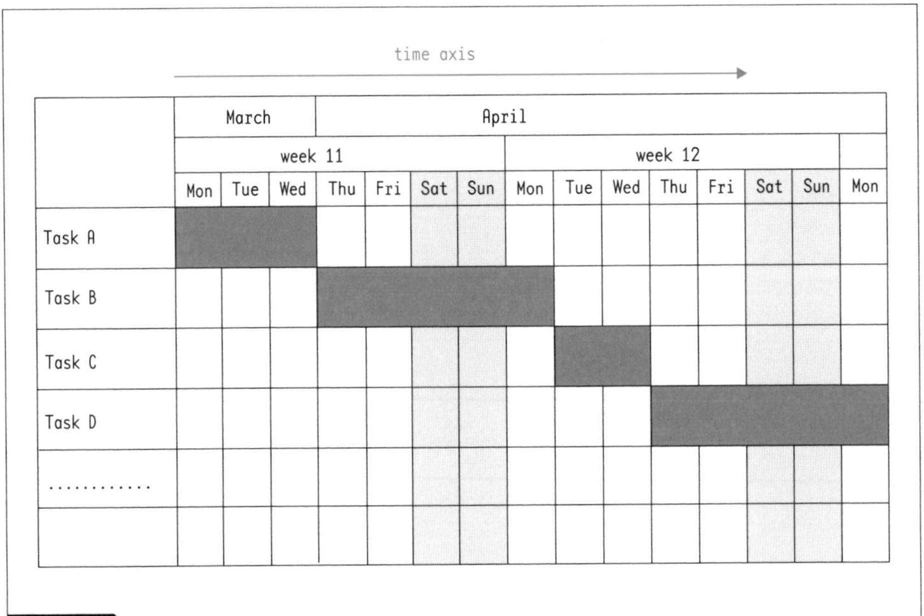

	March			April											
	week 11							week 12							
	Mon	Tue	Wed	Thu	Fri	Sat	Sun	Mon	Tue	Wed	Thu	Fri	Sat	Sun	Mon
Task A															
Task B															
Task C															
Task D															
....															

time axis

Fig.5:
Bar chart principle

_ The space-time diagram, which shows the quantity as a geometric segment (e.g. a stage in highway construction);
_ The quantity-time diagram, which scales the amount to 100% and shows what percentage of the task has been completed, independent of the actual quantity.

The line diagram is generally used less frequently in building construction than in areas involving linear construction sites such as streets, tunnels and sewage systems, in which the construction steps follow each other in regular cycles. In building construction, many tasks, particularly those done by the finishing trades, must be performed in parallel and cannot be clearly illustrated on a line diagram. Nevertheless, the line diagram does have the advantage of being able to represent target-performance comparisons more clearly. › Fig. 6

Network diagram   A network diagram represents scheduled tasks as networks rather than as items along a time axis. Using this form of schedule, planners can effectively map out the reciprocal links between tasks, but it provides only a limited sequential overview of the entire process.

There are three types of network diagrams; the activity-on-node network is the most popular:

16

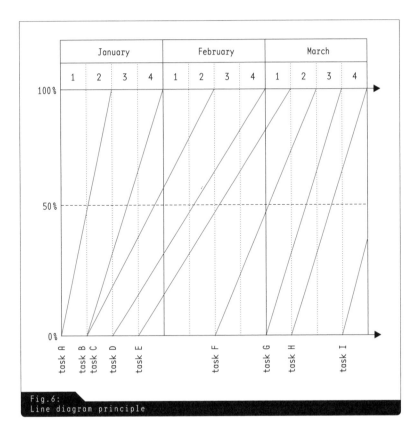

Fig. 6:
Line diagram principle

_ Activity-on-node: Activities are represented by nodes and dependencies by arrows.
_ Activity-on-arrow: Activities are represented by arrows and dependencies by the links between the nodes.
_ Event-on-node: Arrows symbolize the dependencies and nodes represent the results (without durations). › Fig. 7

Network diagrams are rarely used to represent construction schedules, but they are often featured in premium construction scheduling software as an additional means of displaying bar charts. As such, they fulfill an important function in schedule creation. Since they allow for more enhanced graphic representation of dependencies between tasks than a bar chart, planning specialists can switch between these two display modes to better orient themselves within the schedule. Tasks can be recorded and assigned durations using bar charts, while mutual dependencies can be checked and represented using network diagrams.

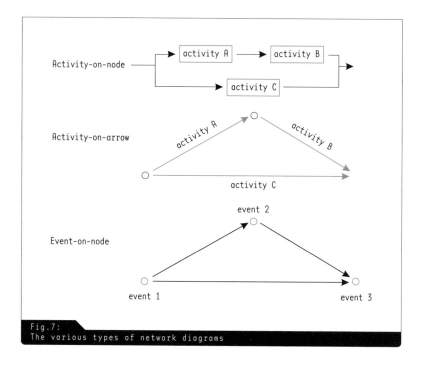

Activity-on-node

activity A → activity B

activity C

Activity-on-arrow

activity A

activity B

activity C

Event-on-node

event 2

event 1

event 3

Fig.7:
The various types of network diagrams

Deadline list

A deadline list is a very simple form of representation. As used in construction scheduling, it presents important deadlines and periods in table form and therefore offers only a limited view of the project. The more deadlines the list contains, the harder it is to read and the more difficult it is for project participants to grasp the interconnections between the individual deadlines.

Deadline lists are often excerpted from the schedule for the different participants in the planning and construction process in order to inform these parties of important deadlines and time periods. Such information may relate, for instance, to the time needed by planners or experts to do their work or to the contractual specifications of the individual contractors. Lists including construction deadlines are often submitted along with tenders, and they may afterwards be incorporated into the construction contract as contractual deadlines. Many scheduling programs can output deadline lists in separate files based on construction schedules.

DEPTH OF REPRESENTATION

A schedule should always meet the specific requirements of the project concerning clarity, functionality and degree of detail. These requirements may vary widely depending on the perspective taken on the

18

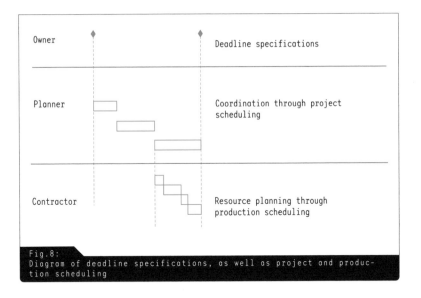

Fig. 8:
Diagram of deadline specifications, as well as project and production scheduling

construction project. There are generally three levels of detail in construction processes, all of which reflect this perspective:

_ The owner's perspective: establishing deadlines with the help of framework scheduling
_ The planner's perspective: coordinating participants with the help of project scheduling
_ The construction contractor's perspective: preparing work and planning resources with the help of production scheduling › Fig. 8

Furthermore, schedules are also categorized in terms of their timeframe (short-term, medium-term, long-term), the person creating them (owner or contractor), and their level of detail (rough, detailed, highly detailed).

Framework schedule

Owners usually have a clear idea of when they want or must begin using a building. A department store may need to be completed by the next Christmas season, or the owner may already have given notice on his or her lease and must be out by a certain date. Planners must take into account the deadlines specified by the owner. Often the financial backers of a project (banks) are also the source of deadline constraints. In order to check the owner's ideas about deadlines and roughly structure the entire process, planners create a framework schedule as an initial overview. It contains the broader sets of tasks and the intermediate deadlines of planning and construction. Typical tasks are: › Fig. 9

No.	Task	Start	Finish	2008						2009											
				J	A	S	O	N	D	J	F	M	A	M	J	J	A	S	O	N	D
1	Project development	July 04, 2008	Aug. 11, 2008																		
2	Planning	Aug. 17, 2008	Jan. 01, 2009																		
3	Building permit	Dec. 12, 2008																			
4	Preparing construction	Jan. 01, 2009	Jan. 15, 2009																		
5	Constructing building shell	Jan. 15, 2009	May 31, 2009																		
6	Finishing work	April 30, 2009	Oct. 30, 2009																		
7	Building services	July 31, 2009	Nov. 11, 2009																		
8	Completion	Nov. 11, 2009																			
9	Inspection	Nov. 15, 2009	Dec. 15, 2009																		

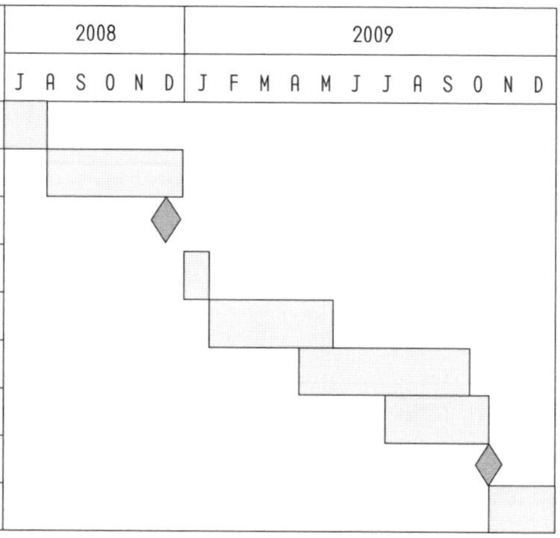

Fig.9:
Example of a framework schedule

_ Project preparation
_ Design
_ Building permit application
_ Preparing for construction work
_ Start of construction work
_ Building structure
_ Building envelope
_ Various finishing jobs
_ Completion

Project
schedule

The project schedule is usually created by the architect, and its objective is to coordinate all the participants in the planning and construction of a building. In order to link the different activities and effectively coordinate the work, the project schedule must have a higher level of detail than the framework schedule. › Fig. 10 The most important factor in combining or separating out tasks is their interdependence. For instance, the building shell often requires a low level of detail since the related tasks are not carried out by different trade contractors and only serve the purpose of deadline control. By contrast, the construction of a drywall may require electrical installations, sanitary installations, door assembly and painting work, which make it necessary to break down the task into several steps. › Chapter Workflows in the planning and construction process, Finishing work As mentioned above, the most effective level of detail in a project schedule generally depends on the project's complexity and timeframe.

20

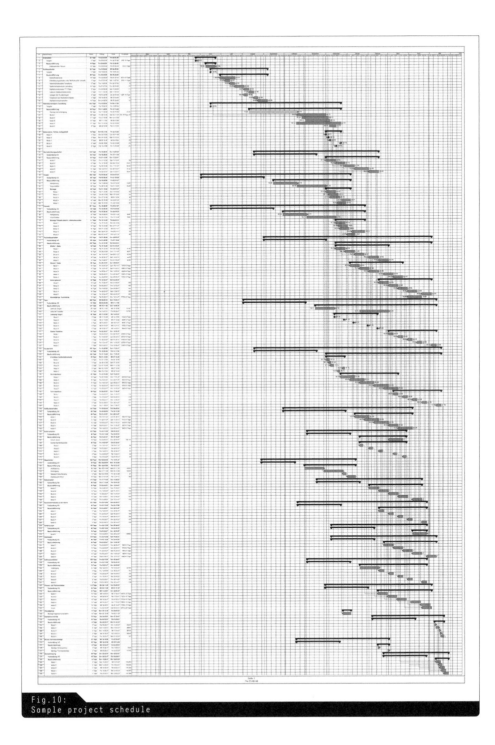

Fig.10:
Sample project schedule

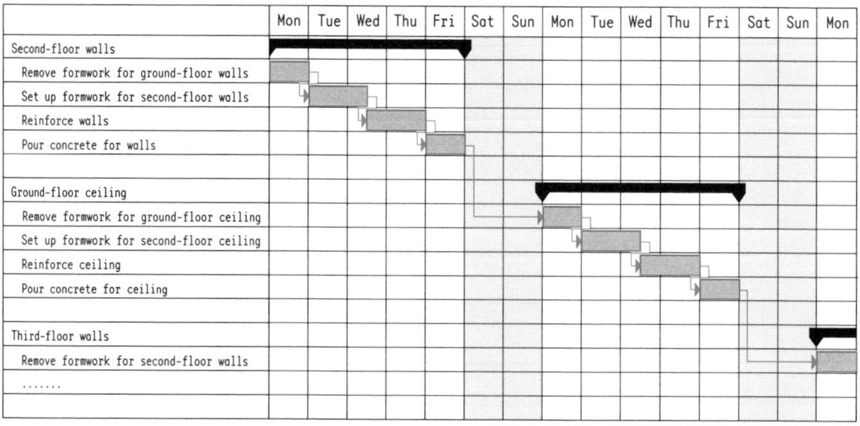

	Mon	Tue	Wed	Thu	Fri	Sat	Sun	Mon	Tue	Wed	Thu	Fri	Sat	Sun	Mon
Second-floor walls															
Remove formwork for ground-floor walls															
Set up formwork for second-floor walls															
Reinforce walls															
Pour concrete for walls															
Ground-floor ceiling															
Remove formwork for ground-floor ceiling															
Set up formwork for second-floor ceiling															
Reinforce ceiling															
Pour concrete for ceiling															
Third-floor walls															
Remove formwork for second-floor walls															
....															

Fig.11:
Example of a repetitive schedule for building shell construction

Moreover, the project schedule should cover the execution of construction work and also integrate the planning phase so that it covers all interfaces. Ideally, the project schedule should be designed in such a way that the various users at the architectural office (construction planning, tendering, construction management) can concisely and clearly display those deadlines that are relevant to their work. › Chapter Workflows in the planning and construction process, Coordinating planning

Production scheduling

Production scheduling has a different objective from project scheduling. While project scheduling is used to coordinate all the project participants, production scheduling is carried out by construction companies to plan personnel, material and equipment resources.

The production schedule adopts deadline specifications from both the framework schedule and the project schedule, and translates them into individual steps in the construction work. This form of schedule enables planners to determine the required number of construction workers and to promptly allocate both equipment and sufficient quantities of material in order to avoid bottlenecks.

The task which the construction company adopts from the project schedule (e.g. a concrete ceiling installed over the ground floor) is broken down into individual steps (placing forms, adding reinforcing steel, pouring concrete, drying, removing forms). It is also assigned the necessary resources. › Fig. 11 Construction companies working on the building shell normally create production plans that can be described as repetitive schedules due to the cyclical nature of the individual work steps. In this case, the construction project is divided into several identical construction phases. Since quantities are identical, companies only need to develop a production schedule for the steps in a single phase and apply it to additional cycles.

Production schedules are used less often in the finishing trades since there are many links between the specialized tasks that place limits on the finishing contractors' ability to organize and schedule the work themselves.

CREATING A FRAMEWORK SCHEDULE

The usual objective of the framework schedule is to examine the feasibility of the owner's deadlines and integrate participants roughly into a plan. When project managers or professional owners participate in larger projects, the framework schedule is often created by the owner and given to planners as a set of parameters.

Deadline specifications from the owner

Depending on the owner's preferences, deadline specifications will take the form of either a directly specified completion deadline or indirectly defined deadlines and periods that participants must observe (e.g. the start of construction in the current fiscal year to give tax advantages). The time span from the start of planning to the completion of the building marks out the framework for the entire planning and construction period.

Dividing the project into planning and construction

Dividing the project into planning and construction periods is a crucial step that allows planners to examine whether both parts of the project can be implemented. While the construction period can usually be streamlined using a cushion and it is also possible to optimize the planning period time-wise, there are limits to such optimization efforts. The two phases must meet basic requirements, and related deadlines can be missed by only a narrow margin.

The start of construction is determined by the availability of the building permit, the related lead times for planning and approval, and the contractual agreement with the construction company. This agreement usually presupposes construction drawings, a call for bids, and the submission of bids from construction companies.

Construction work cannot bypass the typical sequences of the construction process to any significant extent, and there are also limits to the ways it can be organized in parallel sequences.

If a deadline is specified by the owner, the necessary construction period should be calculated backwards from it, or it should be estimated using comparable projects. This approach allows planners to determine when construction needs to start. They must then examine whether planning requirements can be met in the time remaining between the start of the project and the start of construction. Even when making comparisons

23

with other projects, they should always keep the complexity of the project in mind.

If there are grounds for believing that a project is not viable, various alternatives must be considered. For instance, construction time can be shortened by using alternative construction methods (pre-manufacturing, prefabricated parts, materials with short drying times). If the completion deadline is still unrealistic, the problem should be discussed with the owner at an early stage.

Organizing tasks

In addition to dividing the project into a rough planning and construction period, the framework schedule covers a few central planning steps and work sections, presenting them as individual tasks or milestones. > Chapter Creating a schedule, Schedule elements It provides a general overview of the project and ensures that the participants are deployed punctually. Project scheduling generally adds a higher level of detail, but the boundaries are fluid and additionally influenced by the owner's interest in information.

THE STRUCTURE OF THE PROJECT SCHEDULE

Since the project schedule coordinates participants, its rough structure is tailored to their work. The schedule integrates each planner and construction company separately, together with the jobs they do.

Hierarchical structure based on contract work packages

Individual tasks are combined to form <u>summary tasks</u> in order to structure the schedule and create a schedule hierarchy. For example, individual tasks can be assigned to a component group or to a construction phase group. > Fig. 12

The highest hierarchical level should always be the respective <u>contract work package</u>. The term "work package" refers to the construction jobs that have been contracted out in an agreed planning or construction contract. If a work package involves several trade contractors, each must individually be subordinated to the work package. The advantage of this approach is that the hired contractors can be clearly monitored in terms of their individual deadlines and construction jobs. Furthermore, contract

---

\\Example:
It is much easier to evaluate the planning scope and the construction period of a simple hall as opposed to a laboratory building of the same size that will contain sophisticated technical equipment. An additional problem is that a larger number of planners must be coordinated for the laboratory, which increases the risk of disruptions.

\\Tip:
In most scheduling programs, planners can use summary tasks to structure the schedule by "inserting" tasks at lower levels. The respective lower-level task automatically becomes a summary task, the duration of which is determined by the sum of its subordinate tasks.

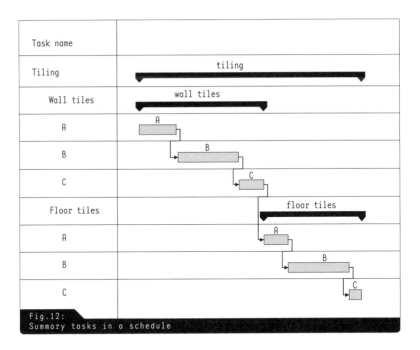

Task name	
Tiling	tiling
Wall tiles	wall tiles
A	A
B	B
C	C
Floor tiles	floor tiles
A	A
B	B
C	C

Fig.12:
Summary tasks in a schedule

award schedules can be created without additional effort and used to establish the deadlines of contract award processes. › Chapter Workflows in the planning and construction process, Coordinating construction preparation, and Chapter Working with a schedule, Updating and adjusting a schedule

Rough phases of an implementation schedule
The work packages are usually arranged in chronological order according to the progress of construction work. If the construction process is divided into segments, it may include the following broad phases:

1. Preparatory measures
2. Building shell
3. Building envelope
4. Interior finishing
5. Building services
6. Final work

Allocating tasks to the work sections
These broad chronological phases can be matched to individual work sections (sometimes with overlaps) in order to produce an initial schedule structure. Afterwards, the construction jobs are categorized under the contract work packages as sets of tasks. › Tab. 1 and Chapter Workflows in the planning and construction process

Tab.1:
Typical work sections in each rough phase

Rough phase	Possible work section
Preparatory measures	– Preparing the construction site (construction fences, construction site trailers, utilities, etc.) – Demolition work – Clearing – Excavating
Building shell	– Excavating – Dewatering – Reinforced concrete work – Masonry work – Structural steelwork – Timber work – Sealing – Ground drainage – Scaffolding
Building envelope	– Sealing – Roofing/roof waterproofing – Plumbing (rainwater drainage) – Windows – Shutters/sunscreens – Facade work (plaster, natural stone, masonry, curtain wall, etc., depending on building envelope)
Finishing	– Plastering – Screed work – Drywall construction – Metalwork (e.g. railings) – Natural/artificial stonework – Tiling – Parquet – Flooring – Painting/wallpapering
Building services	– Ventilation systems – Electrical work – Sanitation/plumbing – Heating/hot water systems – Gas installations – Lightning protection – Transportation and elevator systems – Fire protection – Building automation – Security technology
Final work	– Carpentry (furniture) – Locking systems – Final cleaning – Outdoor facilities

The next steps involve linking the tasks with one another and calculating their duration. › Chapter Creating a schedule, Planning task sequence, and Planning task duration While dependencies in the construction process usually determine the links between tasks, planners should also take outside influences into account. For instance, they might have to observe deadlines specified by the owner or integrate events such as topping-out ceremonies that need to be scheduled before the start of summer vacations. Finally, events taking place in the area around the construction site may have an effect on the schedule (e.g. street or city festivals, utility connection dates specified by the authorities). If at all possible, planners might also find it advisable to schedule critical tasks in a period of more clement weather outside the frost season.

Dividing the work into construction phases is one of the most important steps in organizing the sequence of the different work sections and generally streamlining the schedule. Tasks such as laying floor screed are organized for the different building sections (ground-floor screed work, second-floor screed work, etc.). Smaller phases help produce overlaps between sets of tasks and are advisable since it would "straighten out" the construction process too much if, for instance, the schedule required plastering throughout the building before screed was laid. The tasks are assigned to construction phases in order to inform construction companies where they are to start and in what order the work will proceed. › Fig. 13

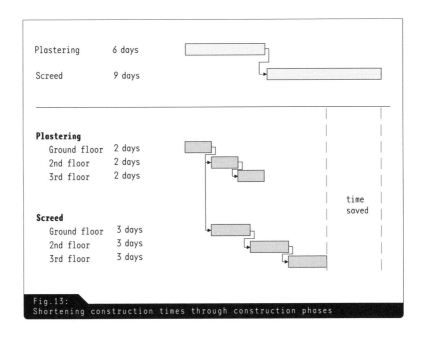

Fig.13:
Shortening construction times through construction phases

27

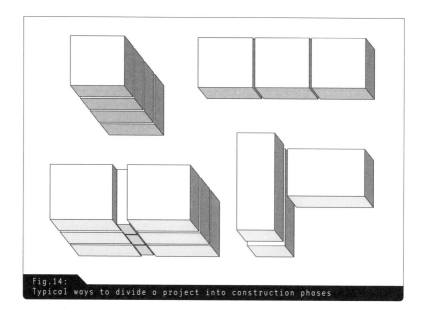

Planners must consider carefully how they divide the project into construction phases when they structure the schedule since changes made to these phases at a later date can result in a great deal of extra work. The rule of thumb is, the smaller the building sections that forms the basis of construction phases, the shorter the construction time. However, depending on the project scope and time constraints, this division must not be too intricate since it is difficult to create a schedule and use it on the construction site if the building has been divided into too many sections. › Chapter Working with a schedule, Updating and adjusting a schedule

While it may not be necessary to divide the smaller projects (home extensions) into phases, large projects may require several phases for the participants to complete construction within an appropriate period.

Finally, the project should also be divided into construction phases that make sense and are easy to communicate. Following the geometry of the building, they can be based on floors, building sections accessed by stairs, units located on both sides of a stairwell, subsequent rental units, etc. › Fig. 14

Important factors to consider for construction phases are separate accessibility, the ability to close off areas, identical production quantities in construction phases, and production processes.

Separate accessibility by means of a stairway or other access route is particularly important for tasks such as laying screed or flooring since it ensures that the different contractors do not get in each other's way

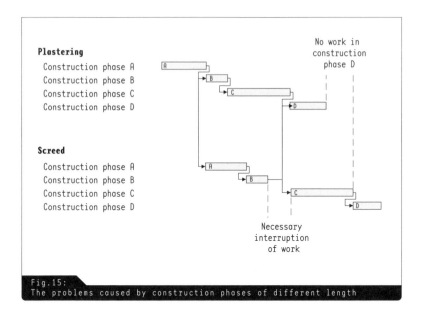

Plastering
Construction phase A
Construction phase B
Construction phase C
Construction phase D

No work in
construction
phase D

Screed
Construction phase A
Construction phase B
Construction phase C
Construction phase D

Necessary
interruption
of work

Fig.15:
The problems caused by construction phases of different length

and are not prevented from reaching their work stations by closed-off areas.

Even so, <u>closing off areas</u> can help to protect completed building sections and surfaces from damage. If areas are closed off or only open to the contractors currently working on them, on-site damage, dirt and theft can be limited, and the responsible party can be identified more easily.

As regards <u>production quantities</u>, planners should define the various construction phases so as to ensure that each phase and work section involves an identical volume of work. This creates continual cycles and avoids long waiting times for the different contractors. › Fig. 15

An additional factor to be considered when dividing a project into construction phases is the various <u>production processes</u> used by the individual contractors. As a rule, a building structure is built floor by floor (from bottom to top), but there are a number of building services contractors that work either along installation paths such as sewage pipes (from top to bottom) or in self-contained cycles (e.g. subdivisions in a rental unit). This is a constant source of misunderstanding and mutual disruptions.

PLANNING TASK SEQUENCE

In order to gain a better understanding of the different tasks, we will systematically follow a single project participant through the typical sequence of the work he or she performs. This sequence can usually be divided into three rough phases:

_ Lead time (necessary planning time, lead time for contract awards and trade contractors)
_ Execution period (planning period or construction, depending on the participant)
_ Lag times (drying and curing times) and follow-up periods

Lead times cover tasks or milestones that must be scheduled before construction work is performed. For example, before windows are installed on site, it may be necessary to take measurements and plan and prefabricate the windows. In contrast, lag times are periods, like drying times, that must be observed after the completion of a task and before additional work can be done on the building section.

Lead time for awarding contracts

Schedulers must take into account the time needed to award a contract, which falls between the planning and implementation period. A basic distinction must be made between private-sector and government procedures. The government usually awards contracts on the basis of strict guidelines or regulations with legally established deadlines. In the private sector, these regulations are not binding. The contract award process can therefore be organized along less formal and more direct lines, yet it should nonetheless adhere to certain minimum periods in order to allow all participants to respond in the proper manner. The deadlines in government regulations are therefore a good foundation for the private sector.

> 🗋
Schedule
milestones

The contract award process involves several steps > Fig. 16 and Chapter Workflows in the planning and construction process, Coordinating construction preparation The schedule should, at the very least, include the following tasks or milestones:

_ Publication, which is necessary for most government procedures
_ Issuing invitations to tender: the deadline by which the planner must complete all documents

🗋

\\ Note:
A lead time for awarding contracts should also be taken into account for planning services in order to find the planning specialists who are best suited and have the most experience for the job (e.g. those with expertise in fire protection for conversions of existing buildings). Public invitations to tender may also be necessary when awarding planning contracts.

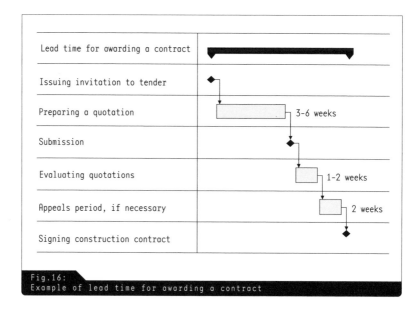

Lead time for awarding a contract	
Issuing invitation to tender	
Preparing a quotation	3-6 weeks
Submission	
Evaluating quotations	1-2 weeks
Appeals period, if necessary	2 weeks
Signing construction contract	

Fig.16:
Example of lead time for awarding a contract

_ <u>Submission</u>: the deadline by which companies must submit their tenders
_ <u>Signing the construction contract</u>: a deadline for the building owner
_ <u>Start of construction</u>

When scheduling the lead time for the award of each contract work package, planners calculate backwards since the lead time is usually scheduled to that construction work begins promptly on site.

The construction contract and the start of construction

A period of at least two weeks must be scheduled between the signing of the <u>construction contract</u> and the <u>start of construction</u> since the contracting company must first make plans before it can begin the construction process (material requirements, transportation to the site, construction site facilities, etc.).

Submission

Sufficient time must also be left between the <u>submission</u> of a tender and the signing of the <u>construction contract</u>—at least one or two weeks, depending on the complexity of the work. During this period, planners examine all the tenders and compile a price comparison list that will be used by the owner as the basis for deciding which construction company to hire. Any unclear items or deviations in the tenders must be discussed with the participants. Government procedures often stipulate an appeals period for bidders who have submitted less favorable offers. The owner's

31

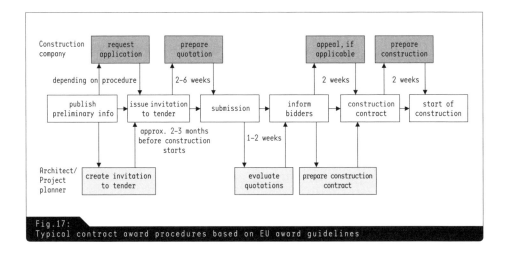

Fig.17:
Typical contract award procedures based on EU award guidelines

decision-making process may at times be arduous, making a period of more than two weeks necessary.

Once the planner <u>issues the invitation to tender</u>, the tendering construction company must put together a <u>solid offer</u> by the submission deadline. Depending on the complexity of the required construction work, the company may require a good deal of time and effort to calculate its offer. It must therefore be given sufficient time to do so—usually around six weeks. The reason for this is that the construction company will have to ask suppliers for their prices or create its own call for tenders in order to get information from subcontractors on sections of the construction work. Even if there is great urgency, construction companies are usually unable to put together a tender in less than two weeks.

Depending on national regulations and the contract award procedure selected, a government agency that contracts out work must publish its intention to award the construction contract in advance. Advance <u>publication</u> of the information enables construction companies to request the tender documents and apply on time. > Fig. 17

Lead times for trade contractors

Not every construction job can be started immediately after the contract is signed. Construction companies must often carry out additional steps before they can perform the work on the construction site. Planners must also take this <u>lead time for trade contractors</u> into account, especially for jobs that require planning work by the contractor, as well as off-site prefabrication and extensive procurement of materials.

To ensure a secure financial framework when <u>procuring materials</u>, companies generally only place orders after signing a contract. For many construction tasks such as plastering and screed work—which use standardized and readily available building materials—companies can do so in the abovementioned two-week period between the signing of the construction contract and commencing construction.

But if companies require materials that cannot be purchased in standard forms at wholesale outlets, planners must consider and check in advance the time involved in <u>planning material requirements</u>.

If the owner wants to inspect samples (e.g. bricks, tiles, windows, colors and similar items) › Figs. 18 and 19 before orders are placed, planners must leave sufficient time for the following steps:

_ Procurement of samples
_ Inspection and approval of samples
_ Modification or procurement of additional samples (if necessary)
_ Material delivery periods

In addition to the time needed to procure materials, some construction work requires planning by the construction company and involves <u>prefabricating</u> components before the work can be carried out on the construction site.

Depending on the construction job, the construction company may have to take on-site <u>measurements</u> in order to prefabricate and install components precisely. Measurements can only be taken once there has been sufficient progress in the construction process (e.g. completion of floors or openings in the building shell).

Based on these measurements, the construction company creates its own <u>working drawings</u>, which provide a foundation for prefabricating the necessary components. If stipulated in the contract, the architect approves technical aspects of the working drawings before components

\\ Example:
In large companies, the staff in charge of construction work may not be able to finalize a decision if contract volume exceeds a certain limit. A higher-level body such as the management board must first approve the contract award. This may entail a long period of time, depending on how often this body meets.

\\ Example:
If natural stone tiles are needed in specific sizes from foreign countries, they must first be ordered, manufactured and imported by ship. If particularly large quantities of a special material or component are needed, or if single parts must be produced, production may take some time due to the lack of supplies at wholesale markets.

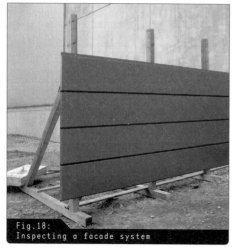
Fig.18:
Inspecting a facade system

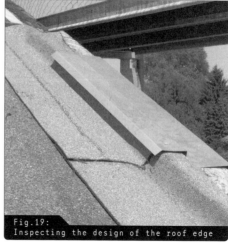
Fig.19:
Inspecting the design of the roof edge

are manufactured. In this case, planners must schedule inspection and approval times in addition to the periods needed to create and work on the working drawings. › Fig. 20

After the architect gives the green light, prefabrication can begin. Depending on the trade contractor and the component, it can take six to eight weeks or more before the component is ready for assembly. However, the actual on-site assembly process usually takes a relatively short amount of time.

Elements that typically require prefabrication are:

_ Facades, windows and doors
_ Glass roofs and skylights
_ Precast concrete units
_ Steel structures (e.g. loadbearing hall structures, stairs, railings)
_ Timber structures (e.g. roof trusses)
_ System elements (e.g. office partition walls)
_ Ventilation systems
_ Elevator systems
_ Built-in furniture and interior installations

Construction period

The construction period encompasses all the tasks covered by the contract work package. When structuring such tasks, planners must consider the dependencies between components and trade contractors, as well as task duration and the assignment of work to construction phases. › Chapter Creating

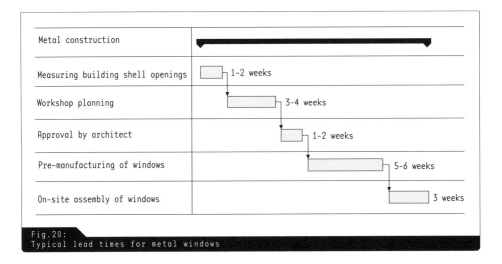

Metal construction	◣━━━━━━━━━━━━━━━◢
Measuring building shell openings	▭┐ 1-2 weeks
Workshop planning	▭━┐ 3-4 weeks
Approval by architect	▭┐ 1-2 weeks
Pre-manufacturing of windows	▭━┐ 5-6 weeks
On-site assembly of windows	▭ 3 weeks

Fig.20:
Typical lead times for metal windows

a schedule, Planning task duration As a rule, the construction company should be allowed to schedule its work on a detailed level if there are no dependencies with other crews. In areas of the building where several trade contractors intermesh, the work should be organized in such great detail that each contractor can see its own working periods and interdependencies.

If the different jobs performed by one trade contractor are separated by longer periods and are not structurally linked, it can be effective to divide the skilled tasks into two contract work packages so that both an adequate planning lead time and self-contained, coherent construction contracts are ensured.

The tasks and dependencies that are typical of the planning and construction process are described in the chapter "Workflows in the planning and construction process."

\\ Example:
Steel and metal construction often involves a number of jobs that extend through the entire construction process. These include the construction of steel structures, windows, exterior wall cladding, doors, railings and stairs. Since in most cases these jobs do not build upon one another and the companies usually specialize in certain fields, it is advisable to plan partially separate contract work packages.

Lag and follow-up periods

These periods can be divided into periods relating to construction work and those relating to contracts.

Construction-related lag times

Of fundamental importance for sequence planning are component curing and drying times, which must be planned as interruptions before additional jobs can begin. Such lag times include <u>curing periods</u> for screed, since screed surfaces cannot bear weight or be walked on directly after pouring. This means that individual areas of the facility are temporarily off limits. <u>Drying time</u> is also needed before additional work can be done on a component. In other words, if tiles, paint or other surfaces are applied to plaster or screed, sufficient drying times must be taken into account so as to prevent subsequent damage to the completed surfaces caused by dampness. In there are many components, curing times and thus accessibility are shorter than the full drying times required before additional work can be performed.

Contractual follow-up periods

<u>Follow-up work</u> that is typically required for individual trade contractors influences the contractually stipulated construction period of a contract work package. Examples of follow-up work are:

_ <u>Building shell</u>: closing wall openings after building services are installed, removing site installations after completion of the building (if contracted out with the building shell)
_ <u>Windows and doors</u>: assembly of windows and door handles before completion of the building
_ <u>Plastering</u>: plastering flush with doors, stair coverings, window sills
_ <u>Building services</u>: detailed installation work for switches, heating elements and sanitary fixtures; launching technical systems
_ <u>Painting</u>: additional coat of paint after tiling, detailed installation work and assembly of fixtures on finished walls and ceilings

Planners should enter such follow-up work into the schedule as separate tasks in order to eliminate the possibility of claims from construction companies that have exceeded contractually defined work times. Also of relevance are the <u>guarantee periods</u> that start with inspections. The sooner both the contractually stipulated work ends and the inspection takes place, the earlier the guarantee periods end that give owners the right to have damage repaired.

Follow-up periods in the field of planning primarily entail information and advisory services that become necessary when designs or conditions change during the construction process (e.g. unexpected discoveries in existing buildings or on the building lot).

PLANNING TASK DURATION

Once planners have recorded all the tasks of the various trade contractors and planning participants, they must now estimate how long tasks will last. Architects usually use empirical values from past projects or question trade associations and construction companies about typical task durations.

Another way to calculate durations is to use defined quantities and quantity-related time values. Here an important distinction must be made between unit production time and unit productivity rate.

Unit production
time

The unit production time (UPT) indicates how many person hours are needed to produce a unit of work. It is calculated as follows:

Unit production time = required person hours / quantity unit (e.g. $0.8 \ h/m^2$)

Unit
productivity
rate

The unit productivity rate (UPR) is the reciprocal of the unit production time. It indicates the quantity produced per time unit:

Unit productivity rate = executed quantity / time unit (e.g. $1.25 \ m^2/h$)

In construction, unit productivity rates are used primarily for equipment (e.g. the performance of a power shovel expressed as m^3/h), while unit production times are applied to labor (e.g. the number of hours needed to make a cubic meter of masonry, expressed as h/m^3).

〉◫
Determining
quantity

Estimations of quantities are based on the quantity units of the underlying unit production times and productivity rates (m, m^2, m^3, or piece). If a productivity rate is expressed in terms of cubic meters of earth, excavations must also be calculated in cubic meters.

Since the quantity units are often the same as those in other stages of the planning process (costing, tendering, etc.), the quantities can be

◫

\\ Note:
Unit production time and unit productivity rate are always dependent on the type of construction company, its working method, and the workers involved. Furthermore, on-site work is often influenced by the specific conditions there. It is therefore never possible to calculate precise task durations in advance using these approximate values.

adopted directly from these other stages. If no quantities are available, they must be calculated from scratch. When choosing the degree of detail in quantity calculations, planners should keep in mind the imprecision of unit production times and unit productivity rates. A rough calculation is normally sufficient.

The total number of work hours necessary to perform a task—known as <u>person hours</u> (PH)—can be calculated on the basis of the required quantity and either the unit production time or unit productivity rate. If person hours are divided by both the number of <u>workers</u> (W) and the <u>daily working time</u> (DWT), the result is the probable <u>task duration</u> (D), expressed in <u>workdays</u> (WD):

$$D = \frac{PH(UPT*quantity)}{W*DWT} \quad D = [WD]$$

The daily working time is usually set by the regulations in collective wage agreements. Overtime must be allowed for in special circumstances, such as significant deadline pressure. All things considered, an optimal number of workers should be allotted so as to ensure an effective construction process. Some jobs such as window assembly require a minimum number of workers—otherwise they cannot be done properly or cannot be done at all. Nevertheless, worker numbers cannot be randomly increased since there is a chance that the workers will then no longer be effectively deployed. One example is screed work, where the number of workers depends heavily on the availability of equipment, the productivity of which can be only slightly increased using more personnel.

The specification of <u>staffing capacity</u> is merely an internal calculation method used to achieve a reasonable implementation duration. Normally planners leave it to the construction companies themselves to deploy an adequate number of workers for the available construction period. However, such calculations can help site managers determine

---

✎

\\ Tip:
Depending on construction conditions, published time values and real values may deviate by up to 50%. Smaller quantity differences in calculations can therefore be seen as negligible. If precise information is required, planners should compare several sources for time values. The appendix contains a summary of many typical unit production times as a basis for calculation.

☌

\\ Example:
If the unit production time is 0.8 h/m², the quantity 300 m², the number of workers 5, and daily work time 8 hours, task duration is:

$$D = \frac{0.8 \times 300}{5*8} = 6 \, WD$$

whether a site is understaffed to the extent that problems will arise in meeting final deadlines. The reverse of the equation can be used to figure out the number of workers necessary to complete a job in the given timeframe.

$$W = \frac{PH(UPT*quantity)}{D*DWT}$$

Such calculations can also be used to evaluate contract awards with reference to the on-site performance capacity of construction companies.

It is an advantage for the scheduler if worker numbers are tailored to task durations in the given construction phase. If several trade contractors work one after the other in one construction phase and then gradually switch to the next phase, identical task durations will ensure that work is constantly being performed in each phase and that crews do not have to wait for each other. › Fig. 21

The results of
duration
planning

It is not necessary to calculate task durations precisely for every single schedule and every single task. Often all that is needed is an estimate based on empirical figures. The main reason is that every construction project is subject to small modifications of task durations, and in most cases these have only a limited effect on the completion deadline for the entire building. What are much more important for meeting overall deadlines are task sequences, which are described in the next chapter. Here errors can cause structural displacements and have far-reaching consequences for the project.

Nevertheless, task durations must not be overlooked since they provide a basis for the implementation deadlines that are agreed upon in the contracts with construction companies. It is therefore crucial to use realistic, viable task durations in order to facilitate smooth execution of the various construction contracts.

\\ Example:
If a total of 240 person hours is required to do a job and the given timeframe is limited to five working days, the number of workers required is calculated by dividing 240 PH by 5 x 8 (PH / D x DWT). The result is 6 workers.

\\ Tip:
When determining task duration, planners should not only take a mathematical approach, but also consider other factors that keep the construction work from proceeding at the same rate as during the rest of the year (holidays, typical vacation periods, frost periods, etc.). This is typical of the time around Christmas and New Year's Eve, despite the fact that a sufficient number of working days are available.

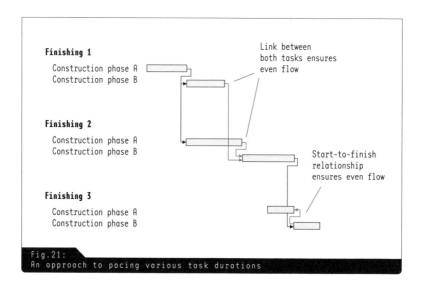

Finishing 1
Construction phase A
Construction phase B

Link between
both tasks ensures
even flow

Finishing 2
Construction phase A
Construction phase B

Start-to-finish
relationship
ensures even flow

Finishing 3
Construction phase A
Construction phase B

Fig.21:
An approach to pacing various task durations

The results
of duration
planning

It is generally impossible to calculate planning services using unit production times, since intellectual and creative work cannot be grasped in terms of hours per quantity unit. The durations of planning tasks are usually determined in conversations with planners and experts when they are hired and as the project progresses. This approach optimally exploits the planners' personal experience and available time. By illustrating the effects of possible delays in planning stages, it also makes the participating parties conscious of their own contribution to completing the project on time.

WORKFLOWS IN THE PLANNING AND CONSTRUCTION PROCESS

The following chapter describes typical tasks performed by the participants in the planning and construction processes and discusses the dependencies of these tasks on one another. Its goal is to use this background information to examine projects, identify relevant tasks and depict them in a real-world schedule.

PLANNING PARTICIPANTS

The various parties that need to be coordinated in the planning phase can be roughly categorized as follows: > Fig. 22

Owners and affiliated parties

To begin with, the owner or client must be mentioned, as the initiator of the building project. The owner may be a single person or a complex web of people and institutions. These different constellations can result in significantly different perspectives on the part of owners, project developers, financial backers (banks), and subsequent users. For example, if the owner is a company or a public institution, the project supervisor must answer to committees and departments that have both influence and decision-making power and that must be integrated into the owner's decision-making processes.

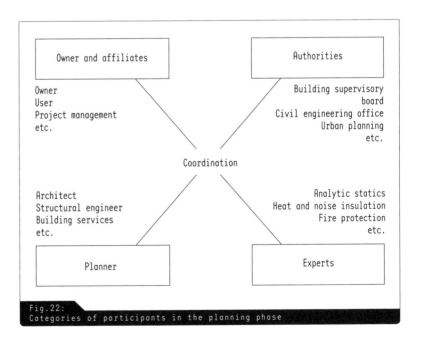

Fig.22:
Categories of participants in the planning phase

In efforts to coordinate the people involved in the owner's company or organization, it is important for planners to understand the decision paths and to estimate the time involved so that they can make punctual preparations for decisions.

› 𝒫

Authorities

Further, every newly erected building requires interaction with the authorities that decide on the legality of the project, grant permits under public law, and monitor the project using tests. The extent to which authorities intervene in the process depends largely on the function of the planned facility, the building type, the legal regulations, as well as local conditions. In addition to building supervisory boards, the project may involve the following authorities:

_ Civil engineering offices (connecting the property to public infrastructure)
_ Urban planning authorities (analyzing the urban planning context)
_ Environmental authorities (the environmental effects of the project)
_ Occupational safety and health authorities (worker safety on the construction site and later in the completed building)
_ Historical preservation offices (for historical buildings)
_ Land surveying offices (maps, site plans)
_ Registry and property authorities (property management, encumbrances and restrictions on the property)
_ Trade authorities (in the event of subsequent commercial use)

Since these authorities normally exercise a control function or serve as decision-makers, planners must understand the steps and durations of their decision-making processes. For example, a realistic time period should be built into the schedule for the authorities to award a building permit—to begin after documents have been submitted.

𝒫

\\ Example:
If, for the additional planning process, architects require an decision from the owner on floor coverings or other surfaces, they should provide the owner at an early stage with samples of viable alternatives with corresponding advantages and disadvantages (costs, lifecycle, sensitivity, etc.). Owners may have to discuss these alternatives with other persons in their organization or with subsequent tenants.

The planning staff consists of various project planners and planning specialists. The project planner (usually the architect) brings them together and resolves any possible conflicts between the different requirements. The three most important integrated planning areas that extend through the entire planning process are the architecture, structural engineering and building services. However, in practice, a large number of planning specialists may be involved:

_ Structural engineering
_ Interior architecture
_ Electrical engineering
_ Drinking and waste water engineering
_ Ventilation systems
_ Fire protection engineering
_ Data technology
_ Elevator engineering
_ Kitchen planning
_ Facade engineering
_ Landscape and open space planning
_ Lighting systems
_ Facility management

Along with the planning participants, experts are required to assess and submit reports on the different specialized tasks. At the very least, this group of experts includes specialists who assess and test heat insulation, noise protection, fire protection and statics.

The experts' assessments must be taken into account in the schedule, primarily in connection with the submission of results. For example, specific expert opinions must be submitted for the construction permit and the start of construction. Experts must therefore be hired and given the work documents with an appropriate lead time.

〉 🗋

🗋
\\ Note:
A detailed description of the participants in
the construction process and of the planning
processes that build upon one another can
be found in: Hartmut Klein, *Basics Project
Planning*, Birkhäuser Verlag, Basel 2008.

COORDINATING PLANNING

The intensity of coordination during the planning phase is very much dependent on the size and complexity of the structure in question and on the scheduling constraints imposed by the owner. In the case of a residential building, which is largely planned exclusively by the architect, only a few deadlines are usually relevant, such as the application and award of the building permit and the start of construction. In larger structures, such as laboratories and specialized production facilities, input from a range of specialists is often required.

The way in which the planning phase is divided up is only partly dependent on the sequence of architectural planning, since other participants will have structured their particular areas differently. The best way to approach the organization of planning is by making an initial link between the three most important planning areas—architecture, structural engineering and building services—since, as a rule, planners in these areas have a constant integrated influence on the planning process as a whole. Planning should take into account the fact that planning specialists require an appropriately advanced state of overall planning in order to be able to make their particular contributions. This networked approach is typified by the following sequence:

1. Advance development of an appropriate foundation for planning specialists by the project planner
2. Forwarded to planning specialists
3. Worked on by planning specialists
4. Results returned by planning specialists
5. Integrated by project planner and coordinated with results of planning by other participants
6. Mutual coordination of specialist planning and (if necessary) further revision

The schedule should allocate enough time after the submission of responses by planning specialists to resolve inconsistencies between specialist planning and project planning or other areas of specialist planning. › Fig. 23

> ✎
> \\ Tip:
> Typical information exchanges between the architect, structural engineer and building services engineer relating to different project phases can be found in the appendix. However, the details of such exchanges differ according to the specific project and depend on the function and design of the building and the people involved.

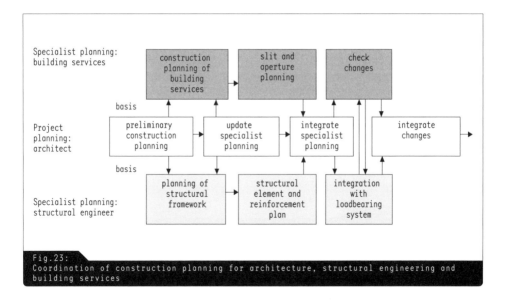

Specialist planning:
building services

| construction planning of building services | slit and aperture planning | check changes |

Project planning:
architect

basis

| preliminary construction planning | update specialist planning | integrate specialist planning | integrate changes |

basis

Specialist planning:
structural engineer

| planning of structural framework | structural element and reinforcement plan | integration with loadbearing system |

Fig.23:
Coordination of construction planning for architecture, structural engineering and building services

<table>
<tr><td>Integration of other participants</td><td>Integrating other participants is generally simpler, since their work is not as closely linked with that of the planners referred to above. It is often sufficient simply to include a period in the schedule in which planning specialists will be given time to react to particular results of the overall planning process. This will clarify when the various participants need to be given the information they require for planning their specific input into the project, and when the results will be integrated into the overall planning process.</td></tr>
<tr><td>Planning milestones</td><td>The most important aspect of the scheduling process is the identification of milestones that can be passed on to the various participants (building owners, planners, experts) in order to provide them with a basis for their respective input into the project. > Chapter Creating a schedule, Schedule elements Established and agreed deadlines ensure that all parties adopt the discipline of a fixed timeframe and help avoid the delays in the planning process that can occur when participants are included in the process too late.</td></tr>
</table>

COORDINATING CONSTRUCTION PREPARATION

When it comes to awarding contracts, planning deadlines must be particularly well thought out. Construction preparation is a time-consuming process that can easily take several months. If it is clear when a building company has to begin work on the construction site, this deadline can be used as a basis for scheduling the different steps in the preparation process. > Chapter Creating a schedule, Planning task sequence If owners are public bodies, legally prescribed deadlines mean that planning can include only limited provisions for delays, which will thus directly affect the start of construction.

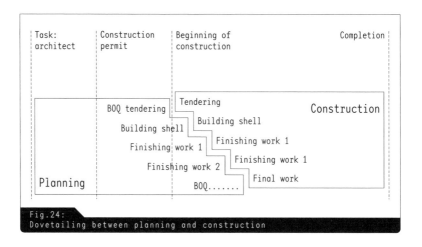

| Task: architect | Construction permit | Beginning of construction | | Completion |

Tendering

Construction

BOQ tendering

Building shell

Building shell

Finishing work 1

Finishing work 1

Finishing work 1

Finishing work 2

Final work

Planning

BOQ.......

Fig.24:
Dovetailing between planning and construction

Since a range of companies are usually involved in a building project, the construction preparation phase must make provision for a range of different deadlines. It is therefore wise to organize the respective steps in the preparation process to ensure that all preliminary work, such as securing owner decisions, construction planning, and organizing and announcing tenders and contract awards, can be punctually initiated in relation to each trade contractor involved.

Dependencies generated by construction workflows also give rise to planning requirements.

Planning during construction

Many rough schedules present planning and construction as separate phases, but in reality, construction planning and construction itself largely proceed in parallel. This is because deadlines are often very tight, and planning does not necessarily have to be completed when building commences. Although it is important that documentation is available in good time before the relevant construction work commences, many types

ρ

\\ Example:
When the building shell is planned, consideration needs to be given to the subsequent effects of facade connections, ceiling and stairwell heights, as well as the surface treatments of concrete walls and their associated requirements. Drainage underneath the bottom slab also needs to be clarified at a very early stage.

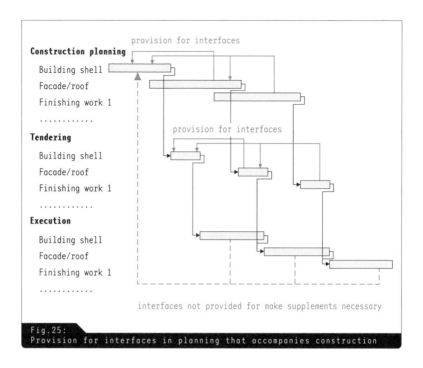

Fig.25:
Provision for interfaces in planning that accompanies construction

of work (such as painting and laying flooring) tend to commence once the building process is quite advanced, which means that relevant planning and contractual documents can be completed after construction has begun. In such cases, owe refer to planning that accompanies the construction process. › Fig. 24

In planning that accompanies construction there is always a risk that specific planning details that are developed later in the process will have an influence on aspects of construction that have already been completed. Many building elements interface with other parts of the building in terms of statics, building services, structure and aesthetics.

Since individual building elements such as windows, doors and dry construction work are increasingly integrated with other work sections, planning for such elements needs to be sufficiently advanced in order to avoid the need for subsequent modifications. › Fig. 25

PREPARING THE CONSTRUCTION PROCESS

During the construction process the building planner or site manager needs to coordinate all companies operating under a separate contract with the building owner. The goal is to ensure that work proceeds in an integrated and trouble-free manner. A central aspect of this coordination involves the

Fig.26:
Manual demolition on projects involving existing buildings

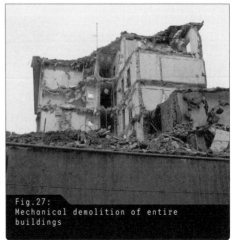

Fig.27:
Mechanical demolition of entire buildings

interfaces between individual tasks and trade contractors. A description of typical interfaces is given below; it should however be remembered that these can vary significantly between different construction projects.

Prior to the erection of the building shell, a number of preliminary tasks relating to the preparation of the construction site need to be considered. First, the site needs to be in a condition that actually allows construction work. Vegetation must to be removed and the ground reinforced, pre-existing piping and drainage systems must be located and protected, and pre-existing constructions (walls, fences, etc.) need to be demolished.

Preparing the construction site

The required preparatory measures include setting up the construction site. This process involves installing the construction trailers from which construction is supervised, connecting utilities, and putting up fences to prevent unlawful entry. Further work may be required to improve access (e.g. access roads) and to shield the site from the external environment (e.g. blinds and noise protection).

Demolition measures

For new buildings, preparatory measures can often be completed within a few days or weeks. However, in projects involving existing building stock, the need for extensive demolition work may require scheduling a significantly longer preparatory phase. At the same time, the unpredictability of the demolition process often makes it extremely difficult to estimate task durations. The choice of the demolition method decisively influences task durations, since mechanical demolition with heavy equipment cannot be compared with manual demolition using light machines. › Figs. 26 and 27 Routes for waste transport within the building and access to dumps also need to be taken into consideration. Because demolition measures precede construction, delays in the demolition phase directly affect all subsequent work.

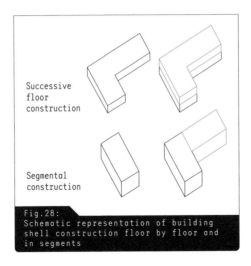

Successive floor construction

Segmental construction

Fig.28:
Schematic representation of building
shell construction floor by floor and
in segments

BUILDING SHELL

Constructing the building shell entails a range of tasks, all of which contribute to creating the building's basic skeleton. In the case of concrete construction these tasks include:

_ Excavation
_ Masonry
_ Pouring concrete
_ Putting up scaffolding
_ Sealing the building to protect against rising damp and groundwater
_ Separate roof construction (if required)

Depending on the type of construction, structural steelwork and timbering may also be needed. As a rule, building shell construction is organized by the construction contractor. Of primary concern for architects are the interfaces with subsequent work sections that commence after the shell has been completed.

The sequence of tasks involved in the construction of the building shell is usually highly structured and easily comprehensible. Once the foundation and drainage systems have been completed, the floors are added in succession. However, where large floor areas are required, building shell construction may involve working in vertical segments as well as successive floor construction. › Fig. 28

Pre-manufac-
turing in the
building shell
phase

If a building is made up of elements such as prefabricated concrete units and steel or wooden structures, these components are usually pre-manufactured off site, delivered ready for assembly and quickly mounted

Fig.29:
Construction of a concrete wall using prefabricated elements

Fig.30:
Construction of bottom slab and concrete supports cast on site

on site. › Fig. 29 and Chapter Creating a schedule, Planning task sequence Apart from the different floors, this usually also applies to roof structures made of wood or steel. These structures may have to be contracted out separately from the building shell, and this needs to be taken into account in the construction schedule.

BUILDING ENVELOPE

Envelope sealed

Directly after the completion of either the building shell (including roof structure) or the individual segments of the shell, the building needs to be sealed off from its surrounding environment. Sealing the building envelope is a basic precondition for all subsequent finishing work. For this reason the "envelope sealed" stage should be reached as soon as possible after completion of the building shell. The relevant functional requirements are:

- Rainproofing (protection for finishing elements, drying out the building shell)
- Windproofing (above all in winter, to retain heat in the building)
- Security (protection against theft of finishing elements)
- Heatability (only necessary during winter months)

Windows and doors

The most important precondition for reaching the "envelope sealed" milestone is the sealing of openings and roofs. This is achieved either by installing windows and doors immediately or by blocking off openings using temporary seals such as guard doors. Depending on the type of construction, builders can add insulation and the facade of the closed external wall immediately after the "envelope sealed" stage. Where additional, thick

50

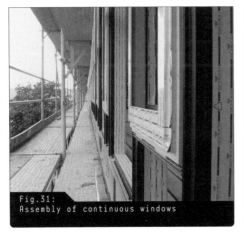

Fig.31:
Assembly of continuous windows

Fig.32:
Assembly in attic area

outer-wall features are added, it may be necessary to modify or shorten scaffolding.

Sealing roofs and drainage

The covering of steep roofs and the sealing of flat roofs must be completed in order to seal the building envelope. This also applies to skylights and roof-light domes and includes the completion of plumbing and roof-drainage work. For drainage embedded within a flat roof, builders must also ensure that once the envelope is sealed, water is actually drained out of the building.

Lightning protection

Before scaffolding for facade and roofing work is removed, lightning protection work also needs to be carried out and lightning conductors must be earthed.

FINISHING WORK

Coordinating finishing work is the most demanding segment of the construction supervision process. Precise scheduling is essential since tasks are closely linked and the different types of work being simultaneously carried out are often not restricted to one or a few companies—in contrast to the building shell and envelope.

Most contractors will not be able to coordinate their own work with that of other contractors because of the complexity involved. For this reason, the schedule must define the relevant dependencies in detail.

Plastering work is generally carried out soon after the building envelope has been sealed. Since in most cases wall installations need to be concealed behind plaster surfaces, they must be in place before plastering begins. In this context care should be taken not to overlook features such as drive mechanisms for doors, fire protection installations and emergency lighting. In industrial buildings, cables are usually laid on the outside of walls, which means that plastering can be done before building services are installed.

Door frames are a typical interface in this context, since the type of door frame chosen determines whether it is mounted before or after plastering. For instance, steel corner frames should be mounted prior to plastering, because embedding frames and intrados later on usually generates additional costs. Dual section closed frames should only be installed late in the construction process to protect against damage. Interfaces that can influence the sequences of all types of work take place wherever building elements intersect with one another, as is the case with windows, window sills, stairway access points and stairway railings. › Figs. 33 and 37, p. 56

In order to ensure that surfaces are ready for further work (e.g. painting), the schedule needs to include a drying period appropriate to the type and thickness of the plaster used.

It is also helpful to include a post-plastering section in the schedule to ensure that surfaces damaged by other work can be repaired at a later date.

Schedules usually make special provision for screed work, because no other work can be carried out while screed is being laid or is curing. As a consequence, the schedule must not only cover screed application but also include a curing period appropriate to the type of material used. Cement screed has a curing time of three to ten days (depending on the aggregate, weather and thickness), and it is significantly more economical than, for example, poured asphalt screed. However, the latter is ready for use and further work after only two days.

Apart from curing time and readiness for use, another important aspect of screed work is drying time. Flooring can commence only after screed has dried sufficiently and moisture content is low. The drying time is primarily dependent on the type and thickness of the screed and on environmental factors such as temperature and humidity. In many cases flooring is only installed late in the construction process to avoid such problems. In cases where deadlines are tight, the drying time can be reduced by using additives or drying equipment, although such measures generate additional costs.

When scheduling screed work, planners should also consider installations laid under screed, such as floor heating, heating distributors, floor power outlets and electrical conduits. › Fig. 34 Due to the inaccessibility of building sections containing freshly applied screed, interconnected workflows need to be checked in terms of possible system bottlenecks, walkways (and escape routes), transport routes for materials, as well as intersecting installation areas (such as electrical conduits).

The sequence in which drywall construction and screed work are carried out also depends on whether more priority is given to noise insulation

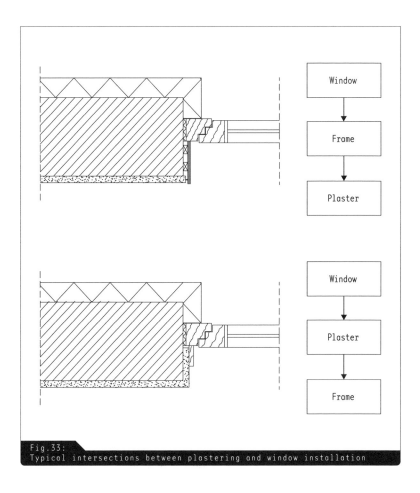

(walls attached to the unfinished floor) or flexibility (walls attached to the screed). Where a large proportion of the walls and ceilings in a building are constructed using the drywall method, the coordination of this work with many other work sections is one of the most important tasks in the scheduling process.

Due to these dependencies, plasterboard walls are usually constructed in two steps. First, the substructure is erected and sealed on one side. This is followed by all installation work related to building services (electricity, sanitation, heating, ventilation). The drywall contractor only seals the second side of the wall once this work has been completed.

The construction of suspended ceilings also involves close integration of installation work and drywalling. All raw installations must be completed before the ceiling is mounted, and planners need to consider possible

Fig. 34:
Installations prior to application of elevated screed

Fig. 35:
Rough installations prior to closing a suspended ceiling

geometric dependencies between installations and the suspension and screening of the ceiling. > Fig. 35

In addition, some building-services elements require specific preparation of drywall surfaces and subsequent sealing once they have been installed (e.g. recessed lighting, access panels, fire detector covers). > Fig. 36

Doors and partition walls

With plasterboard walls, frames are often installed while the wall is being constructed, because they must be screwed to and aligned with lateral profiles. In the case of solid walls, the frame is usually fitted before or after plastering in the form of a corner, profile or dual section closed frame. > Fig. 37, p. 56

In addition to affecting the way doors are mounted (in the building shell and the drywalling work), the type of frame or door construction is a significant factor in determining the point at which mounting should take place. For normal doors, frames are installed before or after plastering or during drywalling depending on the particular situation, and the door leaf is mounted as late as possible to avoid possible damage. Metal frame doors and system elements as well as standardized steel doors and panels are often supplied and installed as complete units, including the frame and door leaf.

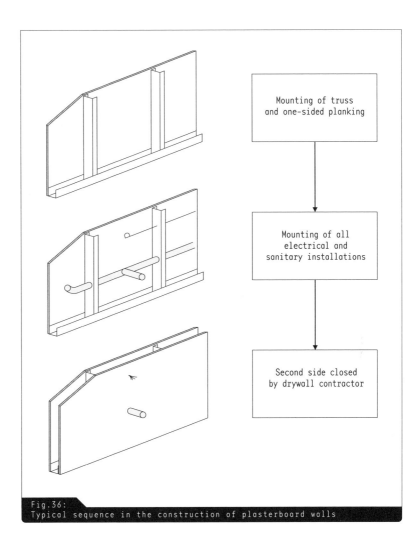

Fig.36:
Typical sequence in the construction of plasterboard walls

Mounting of truss and one-sided planking

Mounting of all electrical and sanitary installations

Second side closed by drywall contractor

In many cases, door details have a decisive effect on the time period allocated for installation:

_ Door frame installation with or without floor recess (dependent on screed)
_ Door structures with or without surrounding frames (dependent on screed)
_ Frame geometry: frame over plaster or plaster applied to frame (dependent on plastering) > Fig. 37, p. 56
_ Permit requirements application of plaster to fire doors

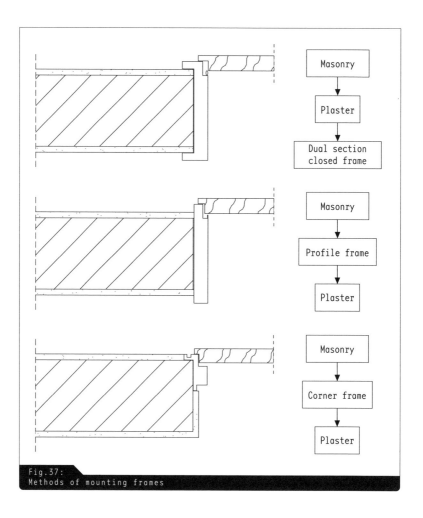

Masonry → Plaster → Dual section closed frame

Masonry → Profile frame → Plaster

Masonry → Corner frame → Plaster

Fig.37:
Methods of mounting frames

_ Electrically operated doors with access surveillance, escape route functions, accessibility for disabled people, automatic door openers (dependent on electrical systems and fire alarm installation)

In principle, sensitive installation elements should be planned as late as possible in order to avoid damage to finished surfaces.

In addition, depending on the type of door, delivery times often must be taken into consideration. Standardized steel doors and frames can be delivered quickly and installed as complete units. Special structures such as fire doors and complete metal-frame door units are manufactured to order, and delivery times can easily be 6 to 8 weeks or more.

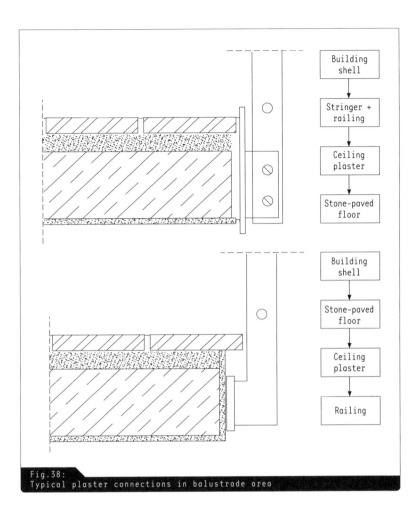

Tiling,
parquet laying,
stonework and
flooring

A fundamental requirement for laying tile and stone surfaces is the completion of the underlying foundation. However, a distinction must be made here between using a thin bed of plaster on a level foundation, and a thick bed on the building shell surface.

Different surfaces, such as screed, building shell surfaces, masking, plaster, drywall etc., can serve as the foundation for all coverings and coatings. For stairs, the sequence in which a covering is applied will also depend on the way the stair railing is attached, the possible addition of a stringer, and in some cases the presence of scaffolding in the stairwell.

> Fig. 38

57

Integrating different surfaces, such as plaster around door frames and different types of flooring, requires careful attention to task sequences. Relevant details need to be clarified in invitations to tender, including bracket and seal requirements. In many areas, particularly bathrooms and kitchens, interdependencies with building services installations need to be taken into account:

_ Sanitation installations: rough installations such as toilet cores, ground outlets, downpipes, water connections, access openings
_ Heating installations: heating pipes, heating elements
_ Electrical installations: switches, floor outlets, etc.

It should be noted that special surfaces such as flooring in elevators and tiled backsplashes in kitchenettes are often overlooked in the planning process.

Wherever possible, floor surfaces should be applied in an order that ensures the least risk of damage. For instance, carpet, plastic and linoleum floors should be installed as late as possible, since they are more susceptible to soiling and damage than parquet, stone or tile. They can also be laid quickly. Laying such floor coverings is often one of the last tasks in the construction process.

Painting and
wallpapering

Painting and wallpapering require dry level surfaces. For this reason, schedules need to include adequate drying times for mineral-based surfaces such as plaster. As a rule, painting and wallpapering work is relevant to all wall and ceiling surfaces that are not covered by other surfaces such as tiles or prefabricated ceiling elements. Planners also need to consider smaller-scale tasks such as the application of varnish to stair rails, frames and steel doors, dust-binding and oil-resistant coatings to elevator shafts prior to elevator installation, and fire- and rust-resistant coatings to steel structures. As with plastering, provisions should be made in the schedule for follow-up work.

> ♀

♀
\\ Example:
Heating elements represent a typical interface problem. Planners need to be aware that heating is required on the construction site over the winter months in order to ensure that sub-surfaces and paintwork dry properly. However, in some cases heating elements must be removed again later on, to allow the wall areas behind them to be painted.

BUILDING SERVICES

Building services include all installation work involving heating, water supplies and drainage, sanitation units, ventilation, electrical installations, data technology, fire prevention installations, elevators and other building-specific installations. Coordination of building services and their integration with interior finishing work are generally based on collaboration between building and building services engineers. In this context, it is important that building planners understand where the interfaces are located between different building services contractors and integrate these interfaces into workflows. > Fig. 39

Heating
installation

Heating installation involves a range of different construction elements. The order in which these elements are installed during a particular project must be determined on the basis of the different systems and distribution networks. Typical elements are:

_ Energy supply (gas pipes, solar collectors, pipes, etc.)
_ Storage facilities (e.g. hot water and oil tanks)
_ Heat stations and heat generation
_ General distribution and sub-distribution within the building (duct installations)
_ Distribution per heating unit (heating unit connection)
_ Heating unit installation

Planners need to coordinate the installation of the heating system with relevant interior finishing work on a range of surfaces. If the heating system is to be used to heat the construction site during the winter months, parts of the system need to be installed in advance and then temporarily removed to permit work on surrounding surfaces (plastering and painting).

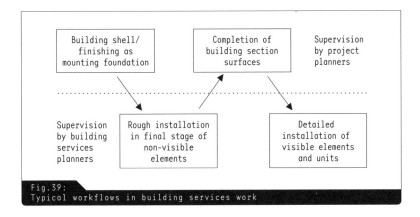

Fig.39:
Typical workflows in building services work

Like heating systems, sanitation systems require closed and some-times pressurized circuits and networks. For this reason, the workflows involved are similar to those in the installation of heating systems. Apart from the connection of the building to the local water provider, planners dealing with the installation of the drinking water supply need to understand how it is distributed throughout the building via feed pipes, ascending pipes in installation shafts or wall slits, and connections to individual use points in bathrooms, kitchens and similar rooms. Analogous planning must be performed for sewage disposal.

> 🛈

The rough installation phase is followed by the detailed installation of sanitation facilities (sinks, toilets, faucets, etc.). This work is often scheduled well after the completion of tiling and painting work > Fig. 41 in order to avoid the risk of theft or damage. Elements such as bathtubs and shower trays that are to be tiled on the outside need to be installed before tiling work commences.

Typical interfaces requiring coordination between work sections:

_ Piping underneath the bottom slab (often installed during building shell construction)
_ Wall and ceiling openings (which in some cases need to be closed after installation during building shell construction)
_ Ventilation ducts running through the roof (connection of sewage disposal pipes to fans in the roof area)
_ Water and sewage connections to the building (requiring coordination with public providers)
_ Installation of pumping systems below the backwater level
_ Heating water (installed centrally with a parallel piping configuration or decentrally at the point of use)

Electrical installation work is also divided into rough and detailed phases. Depending on the method used, rough installations can be concealed beneath plaster or left exposed. If, as in residential buildings, cabling is not supposed to be visible, completion of the entire electrical network must be scheduled between the building shell and plastering phases. The visible (exposed) mounting often encountered in industrial buildings

🛈
\\ Note:
Further information on drinking water and sewage system components can be found in: Doris Haas-Arndt, *Basics Water Cycles*, Birkhäuser Verlag, Basel 2009.

Fig.40:
Drinking water and sewage installations
in the toilet core with hollow floor

Fig.41:
Tiled surface ready for detailed
installation of sanitation facilities

is usually carried out only after all wall surfaces have been finished. Exposed concrete walls are a special case, in that ductwork must already be laid in the wall when it is reinforced in order to allow for later electrical installations. › Fig. 42 Typical stages in electrical work are:

_ Building connection and main fuses (coordination with electricity provider)
_ Earth connection (coordination with building shell work)
_ Battery and transformer installations (if required)
_ Distribution within building and sub-distribution to individual points
_ Detailed installation of lights, outputs, switches etc.

Due to the increasing integration of structural elements with electrical systems, scheduling electrical work is becoming an increasingly complex task. In order to avoid having to open finished surfaces for additional installation, planners need to systematically check construction elements detailed in the building design for possible interfaces with the electrical system. Typical examples are:

_ Specific connections for stoves, tankless water heaters, heating systems and particular structural elements
_ External lighting
_ Emergency lighting
_ Fire alarm units
_ Ventilation units
_ SHEV units (window, roof opening, smoke extraction)

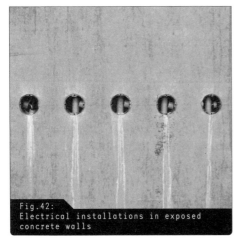

Fig.42:
Electrical installations in exposed
concrete walls

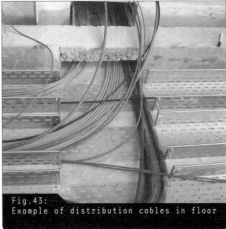

Fig.43:
Example of distribution cables in floor

_ Disabled access (switches, automatic overhead door closers) and access monitors
_ Alarm system components (outer doors and emergency exits, window burglar alarms, surveillance cameras, etc.)
_ Facade control (electrical ventilation, sun and glare protection, rain and wind detectors, overhead lights, etc.)

Data technology   Data technology is a special aspect of electrical installation and is particularly complex in buildings used for administration and communications. Data technology refers to all forms of telecommunications and media technology such as telephone connections, television technology, computer networks, server rooms, etc.

In order to provide flexible access to every workstation in administrative buildings, server rooms and wiring closets are often installed either centrally or on each floor. Planners need to take into account dependencies with installation channels in floors, ceilings and walls.

Ventilation   Planning the installation of ventilation or air-conditioning systems
systems   must also cover the installation of extensive ductwork for incoming and outgoing air. As a rule, ventilation ducts, whether exposed or concealed, are laid in shafts, floor structures and ceiling areas, and planners must ensure that such installations are properly integrated with relevant structures and surfaces. It is critical in this context to take into account aspects such as supply conduits (cooling pipes, electrical cables, inlet vents), penetrations from the outer surface (caulking by roofer or facade construction contractors) and fire compartments (mortaring by the building shell contractor or fire-retardant sealing by the drywall contractor).

Along with the individual interfaces between the distribution system and the ventilation plant, the schedule for later work in the construction process needs to accommodate the detailed installation of features such as exhaust outlets, grating, covers and screens. Such installation is generally carried out after surfaces have been finished.

An important consideration when scheduling the installation of large ventilation and air-conditioning systems is lead time for prefabrication. Apart from a few standardized duct cross-sections, the dimensions of ducts, intersections and units must usually be calculated on site during building shell construction and represented in an independent working drawing. The components are only manufactured once this drawing has been approved, and the entire process can take several weeks. It is therefore important that the ventilation system contract be awarded to a specialist company at an early point so that the work on the building site can be carried out punctually.

Transportation technology

Conveyor technology such as elevators and escalators usually requires a large number of electrical connections. Planners also need to take into account interfaces with floor coverings (inner covering of an elevator car, connection to door sills) and walls (elevator door embrasure).

In most cases, the anchorage points for a planned elevator must be defined by anchorage channels already installed within the shaft during the building shell construction phase. This enables planners to select the elevator construction contractor or manufacturing system at the earliest possible stage. Once the building shell has been completed, the shaft is measured precisely, and a working drawing for the elevator is made. Following the pre-manufacturing phase, installation often proceeds in several steps. First the load-carrying system is installed in the shaft, then the elevator car is mounted, and finally the electronic control system is put in and connected with the electrical system.

Scheduling also needs to consider whether the elevator will be used to transport materials during subsequent construction. However, such use of elevators is usually not advisable because damage to the interior of the elevator car is inevitable. As a result planners often make a conscious decision to complete all work on elevators in a late phase of construction.

FINAL WORK

Final contract awards prior to completion

Apart from the follow-up work by individual participants already referred to (painting, detailed installation etc.) there are also entire sets of tasks that are concluded only at the end of the construction process. These can include:

_ Final cleaning following the completion of all work and prior to handover to users

_ Locking systems (delivery and installation of the final locking and access systems for later users)
_ Completion of outside space (access routes, garden and lawn design, parking areas, signage, lighting and other outdoor installations)

Inspections
stipulated by
law

In principle it is wise to schedule in a period at the end of a project for the correction of defects and for formal inspections, since these take time and inspection should be completed before the occupation date.

Inspections include both contractually stipulated inspections and inspections as prescribed under public law. In the latter case the building supervisory board checks that the completed building observes construction regulations, and approves the building for use. Such inspections also cover technical installations such as fire prevention facilities and heating and air-conditioning systems, which in some cases have to be checked by outside experts.

WORKING WITH A SCHEDULE

Even though a schedule may present a detailed and coherent arrangement of the tasks making up a construction project, it is not a static framework that, once formulated, will necessarily remain unchanged until the completion of work. The construction process continually gives rise to particular situations that make it necessary to adapt the deadline structure. A construction schedule should therefore be seen as a tool that accompanies the entire construction process.

UPDATING AND ADJUSTING A SCHEDULE

Conception versus reality

Real conditions on a construction site often look different from the situation envisaged in the schedule. There are many reasons for disruptions and necessary structural changes. › Chapter Working with a schedule, Disruptions to the construction process Schedules, which are usually printed on paper and displayed on the construction site, age quickly, resulting in work that no longer reflects their constraints. This makes updating the schedule essential. Ideally, a schedule is not seen as a set of imposed obligations that need to be repeatedly adapted to the actual construction situation, but as a daily tool that helps planners monitor, organize and, if necessary, adapt the actual construction process.

Structuring the schedule

When formulating a schedule, planners should therefore structure it in a way that allows them to make effective and sensible adjustments and additions during the construction process. In large-scale projects, schedules are often confusing due to the range and complexity of the tasks involved. In such cases the individual tasks should be hierarchized using a clear structure of summary tasks. › Fig. 44 This enables the construction phases and workflows to be presented in detail and also to be seen within the overall deadline structure.

User-oriented schedule versions

This approach makes for easier comprehension of the schedule in its entirety. It can also be represented in different ways depending on the specific user. Typical modes of displaying the schedule include:

_ Overview for project manager and clients: shows major summary tasks; does not show individual tasks
_ Planning and contract award deadline schedule for the planning office: shows all individual planning tasks and award lead times: does not show construction tasks
_ Construction schedule for site managers: does not show planning and award lead times; shows all contractor lead times and construction tasks
_ Construction schedule as a guide for individual participants: shows the participant's tasks only

65

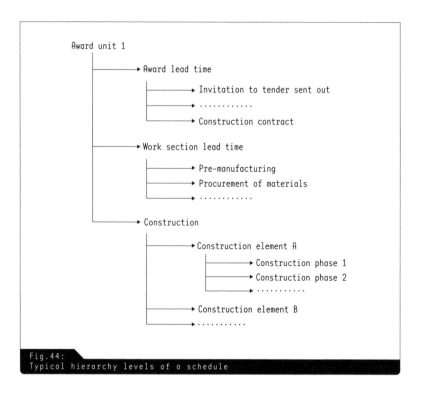

Award unit 1
    →Award lead time
            →Invitation to tender sent out
            →. . . . .
            →Construction contract
    →Work section lead time
            →Pre-manufacturing
            →Procurement of materials
            →. . . . .
    →Construction
            →Construction element A
                    →Construction phase 1
                    →Construction phase 2
                    →. . . . .
            →Construction element B
            →. . . . .

Fig.44:
Typical hierarchy levels of a schedule

By showing only those tasks that are relevant to a particular target group, the schedule provides a clear basis for participants in terms of planning and execution.

An important criterion for the relevance of all modes of display is that they be based on a single coherent schedule. If different schedules are used in parallel, the various users and multiple influences make synchronization difficult at a practical level. Integrating modifications from a single point and then passing them on to all participants using the hierarchical structure described above facilitates their application to the relevant parts of the overall process.

Integrating modifications

Apart from hierarchization, the usability of a schedule in practice is greatly improved when planners establish a clear connection between all sets of tasks. Identifying the effects of a modification requires the integration of all the tasks into a single context that allows the entire schedule to be updated automatically. At the same time it should be noted that not every delay or adjustment affects the deadline for completion.

Critical path

Usually there is only one dependency running through the project from start to finish—a dependency that, if subject to delays, has an immediate effect on the deadline for completion. This is referred to as the

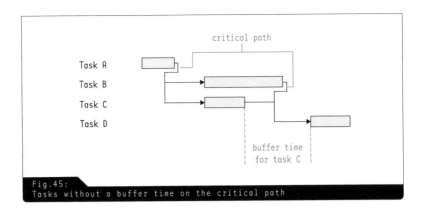

critical path

Task A

Task B

Task C

Task D

buffer time
for task C

Fig.45:
Tasks without a buffer time on the critical path

critical path. In the case of other tasks, a <u>buffer time</u> can be used to prevent delays influencing the critical path. › Fig. 45

Buffer time

Every task that is not on the critical path has a buffer time that can be calculated by modern scheduling programs. This means that planners can directly monitor the degree of flexibility at their disposal when faced with a potential delay, and also see how much additional time they can allow the construction contractors involved.

DISRUPTIONS TO THE CONSTRUCTION PROCESS

Most of the modifications planners find it necessary to make to a construction schedule are based on disruptions to the construction process. Disruptions can be caused by clients (owners and planners and construction firms contracted by them), contractors or by third parties.

Disruptions
from the client
side

Typical examples of disruptions from the client side are:

_ <u>Changes made by the owner</u>: owner requests retroactive changes based on new user specifications, structural alterations to planning etc.

\\Tip:
Using colors, bar formats and hatchings to distinguish individual tasks, milestones, summary bars and entire construction areas improves a schedule's legibility. These features make individual work sections and construction phases easily identifiable. Automatic labeling of summary bars and tasks is also helpful.

\\Tip:
Calculating buffer time has an additional advantage. If there are no links between tasks in the subsequent phases of construction, the buffer time extends to the final project deadline. The scheduler can easily check longer buffer times to ensure that possible dependencies have not been overlooked.

– <u>Lack of contribution by client</u>: failure to give approval, non-payment etc.
– <u>Mistakes by planners contracted by client</u>: mistakes in planning, planning not submitted in time, incomplete calls for tenders, unrealistic schedule, insufficient construction supervision etc.
– <u>Mistakes by contractors engaged by client</u>: preparatory work is not completed in time and the client is therefore unable to make the site available to contractors.

Disruptions by
the contractor

Different events can also lead to disruptions caused by contractors. In the worst case, a contractor becomes insolvent and is forced to declare bankruptcy. The client is then forced to find and engage a new contractor to complete the remaining work, which causes significant delays to the construction process. On the other hand, construction firms that have taken on a large number of contracts often have problems meeting their contractual obligations with the workforce at their disposal. This can produce delays on the individual construction sites. Strikes and flu epidemics, for example, can also significantly reduce the number of staff that construction firms can allocate to a particular contract.

Capacity
problems

Capacity planning is often also faced with problems. Construction firms plan their staffing capacities at regular intervals (e.g. weekly) and allocate their available workforce across different construction sites. Firms cannot usually vary the size of the workforce they allocate to individual construction sites from day to day. If schedules demand daily variations in workforce provision, there will be a high probability of disruptions.
> Fig. 46

For this reason, in order to avoid problems at a later stage, planners should endeavor to schedule work sections in way that allows staff capacity to remain relatively constant.

Disruptions by
third parties

Apart from clients and contractors, third parties contractually engaged in the construction process can also cause disruptions. These can

\\Tip:
In order to ensure that firms have a constant level of work, tasks are linked not only to other job areas but also to one another within the same work section. This allows schedulers to preplan a range of teams that can successively work on individual aspects of the same work section.

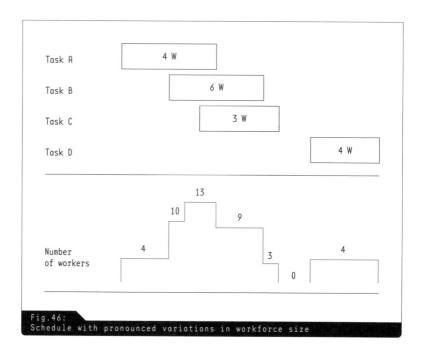

Fig. 46:
Schedule with pronounced variations in workforce size

range from constraints and conditions imposed by authorities, strikes, and theft of clients' and contractors' property, to force majeure. If disruptions by third parties influence the client's situation, contractors have the right to claim an appropriate extension of the time scheduled for construction. If the influence of third parties affects the contractor's level of risk, the construction firm in question is nevertheless obliged to meet its obligations punctually. In the case of force majeure such as storm damage, flooding etc., the construction firm is usually granted a time extension.

> Tab. 2

Effects of
weather

Even in large-scale projects, unfavorable weather conditions in the winter months and other times of the year often lead to delays in meeting schedules. Although declines in performance over the winter months or in holiday periods can generally be offset by longer buffer times and task durations, predicting winter weather conditions precisely is impossible. Depending on the location of the construction site, frost and other adverse conditions can bring construction to a standstill for a long period. Early installation of heating or site-heating facilities can remedy this situation. However, planners need to note that, despite adequate temperatures inside the building, materials such as ready-mixed concrete, poured asphalt and ready-mixed plaster cannot be applied if external temperatures are too low.

Tab.2:
Contractual consequences of disruptions for construction process

Influence of the client (CL)	Influence of the contractor (CN)	Example of influence	Can CN claim time extension?	Can CL claim additional payment?
Direct	No	Directive by the CL, e.g. work stoppage due to lack of funds, or changes to construction	Yes	Yes
Indirect	No	Lack of CL involvement, e.g. late submission of approval	Yes	Yes
Indirect	No	Third-party influence on CL, e.g. preparation delays mean site not be ready for construction work	Yes	Yes
No	No	Force majeure, e.g. storm, war, environmental disaster	Yes	No
No	Indirect	In-house disruption to CL, e.g. flu epidemic or strike	No	No
No	Indirect	Third-party influence on CL, e.g. theft or equip-ment	No	No
No	Direct	Refusal to fulfill contract, e.g. too few workers on site	No	No

Types of disruptions

Disruptions relevant to the schedule can basically be divided into three categories: › Fig. 47

_ Delayed completion: A task begins at a later time but is completed within the prescribed task duration.
_ Extended construction time: A task requires longer than the planned task duration.

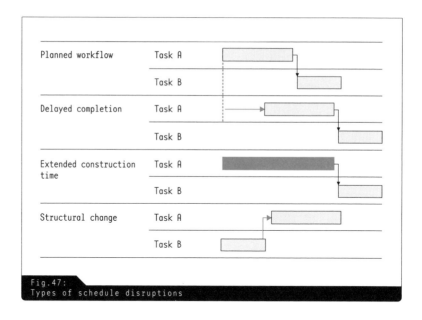

Planned workflow	Task A
	Task B
Delayed completion	Task A
	Task B
Extended construction time	Task A
	Task B
Structural change	Task A
	Task B

Fig.47:
Types of schedule disruptions

_ Structural change to the construction sequence: The construction process, or rather, the interdependent tasks, are arranged in a sequence that differs from the one planned.

DEALING WITH DISRUPTIONS

Should disruptions occur that require "critical path" intervention due to structural changes or because they could cause the project to miss its completion deadline, planners must endeavor to deal with these problems within the prescribed construction period. Possible forms of intervention include:

_ Checking necessary dependencies
_ Structural changes in the construction process
_ Changing the method or quality of construction
_ Shortening construction phases
_ Accelerating construction work

Necessary dependencies

Not every dependency is absolutely necessary, even if it makes sense. Work can sometimes be done retroactively if sufficient consideration is given to the subsequent tasks and if the connections to other components can be subsequently reworked.

Planners must first check whether a dependent relationship is compulsory with an eye toward additional work steps (plastering → painting), or whether they can organize the work in other sequences. It is probably best to discuss any related problems with the participating construction companies.

Structural
changes

If it is impossible to avoid interventions in obligatory dependencies due to the scope disruptions and the need to meet the completion deadline, planners need to consider the possibility of structural changes to the construction process. If there are many consecutive tasks, it is possible to change the structure of components. For instance, light partition walls can be installed on an unfinished floor or on finished screed, and electrical lines can be laid beneath or over plaster. As a rule, though, these decisions must be discussed with construction companies and the building owner since they often influence the properties and visual impression of the completed component.

Method and
quality of
construction

Schedules can be partially streamlined by changing the method and quality of element construction. This may avoid long lead times in the pre-manufacturing process and long curing and drying times.

Shortening
construction
phases

One method of process optimization is to shorten the construction phases. As described above › Chapter Creating a schedule, The structure of the project schedule construction periods can be reduced if back-to-back work is organized into cycles. If the first contractor completes work on a floor only after the next contractor begins, more construction time is needed than if the floor is divided into smaller construction segments. In the latter case, one or several contractors can work on the floor at the same time. In case of doubt, a delayed contractor must be called upon to finish parts of the construction area in order to allow the subsequent contractor to start work there.

\\ Example:
Work that produces a lot of dirt such as plastering, laying screed or putting in cut stone floors, should be scheduled before jobs such as carpeting and painting where surfaces are easily soiled. This is not to say that a stairway cannot also be laid with stone at a later stage in a project as long as areas with carpeting are closed off until the stone work has been completed and the stairway has been cleaned.

\\ Example:
If planners are confronted with tight deadlines and wish to avoid curing and drying times for a cement screed and thus work holdups in the areas in question, they can, as an alternative, install poured asphalt or dry screed, which can be walked on one day later. It should however be noted that this is more expensive than cement screed.

In general, the client may ask a contractor to work more quickly, but distinctions must be made between the causes of the delay. If the contracting company is responsible, it must take all the necessary measures—including overtime and deployment of additional workers—in order to meet the agreed deadline, and it must do so on a cost-neutral basis. However, if the client or the site manager requests a third company that is not responsible for the delay to speed up work, the client must pay for any additional costs.

Since the measures described above often produce additional costs, the owner must be involved in the decision-making process. It is ultimately the owner who must decide what funds he or she is prepared to mobilize to ensure that the building is completed on time.

Even in the initial phase of creating the schedule, planners are well advised to integrate delay periods. Problems almost always arise—insufficient preliminary work, delivery delays, theft of materials, etc.—and they will have to be dealt with. The time cushions in a schedule are an important way to ensure completion deadlines are met. If no cushion exists when planners create a schedule, it is usually a sign that the completion deadline is unrealistic.

Furthermore, at an early stage in the project, planners should also consider the latest point at which they will still be able to select an alternative construction method without violating the contract or incurring additional costs (e.g. cast-in-place concrete vs. prefabricated solutions, plaster vs. plasterboard, cement screed vs. dry screed, plaster flush with doorframes or closed frames). The deadline conditions should be analyzed in good time, and corresponding decisions discussed with the owner.

SCHEDULING AS PROCESS DOCUMENTATION

Scheduling is not only a method for organizing the construction process. It also performs an important function in documenting the project. Since it evolves over the entire planning and construction process, it can be used in retrospect to prove or disprove the occurrence of disruptions. This is important if there are unresolved claims between the owner and construction companies (e.g. compensation for damages) that need to be settled. Further, the schedules of completed projects are a source of data for future schedules and therefore represent important knowledge gained by the planning architect in the process.

The main task of scheduling in this context is to record actual task durations as compared to the target task durations estimated by the scheduler. Disruptions and their causes should also be jotted down. One method is to document current events on the construction site by making handwritten entries into the current schedule. The paper copies, which should be filed at regular intervals, provide a basis for updating the schedule. Ideally, site managers will enter the deadlines directly into a scheduling program that will keep the schedule data constantly up to date. However, after each change, the previous version and its associated data should be archived under the proper date.

IN CONCLUSION

Complex building projects require a great deal of organization and coordination. Without solid scheduling, it is impossible to achieve effective time management of large construction projects. For both the architect in charge of this coordination and the site manager, it is extremely important to organize all the planning and construction processes in advance in order to remain in control of the situation. If these parties only respond to events and are unable to actively control the process, the self-organizational attempts of project participants will often result in disruptions, coordination problems, mutual interferences and delays.

Nevertheless, managing the planning and construction processes is not a matter of giving project participants written-in-stone deadlines that they must strictly follow. Planning specialists must consider all their concerns and integrate them into the management process in order to find solutions that everyone can implement.

A schedule is not merely a contractually agreed service between the building owner and the architect. It is also an effective instrument for the daily management of planning and construction processes. The creation of a realistic and implementable schedule involves effort, but keeping the entire planning and construction process in mind, planners will find that it makes later coordination and conflict resolution a good deal easier. It also lays the groundwork for short construction periods. The more architects devote themselves in advance to sequences in the construction process, the easier the work of site managers becomes.

APPENDIX

LITERATURE

Bert Bielefeld, Thomas Feuerabend: *Baukosten- und Terminplanung*, Birkhäuser Verlag, Basel 2007

Tim Brandt, Sebastian Th. Franssen: *Basics Tendering*, Birkhäuser Verlag, Basel 2007

Chartered Institute of Building (ed.): *Planning and Programming in Construction*, Chartered Institute of Building, London 1991

Wilfried Helbig, Ullrich Bauch: *Baustellenorganisation*, Rudolf-Müller-Verlag, Cologne 2004

Hartmut Klein: *Basics Project Planning*, Birkhäuser Verlag, Basel 2008

Werner Langen, Karl-Heinz Schiffers: *Bauplanung und Bauausführung*, Werner Verlag, Neuwied 2005

Richard H. Neale, David E. Neale: *Construction Planning*, Telford, London 1989

Jay S. Newitt: *Construction Scheduling. Principles and Practices*, Pearson Prentice Hall, Upper Saddle River, NJ, 2009

Lars-Phillip Rusch: *Basics Site Management*, Birkhäuser Verlag, Basel 2008

Sandra Christensen Weber: *Scheduling Construction Projects. Principles and Practices*, Pearson Prentice Hall, Upper Saddle River, NJ, 2005

Falk Würfele, Bert Bielefeld, Mike Gralla: *Bauobjektüberwachung*, Vieweg Verlag, Wiesbaden 2007

INFORMATION REQUIRED FOR PLANNING

Tab.3:
Information typically required by the main planner in the initial project phase

From:	To:	Required information
Structural engineer	Architect	_ Relevant structural systems and materials _ Full range of component dimensions
Building services engineer	Architect	_ Type of installations required for building use _ Location of utility and wiring rooms _ Route of main lines, required routes for main distribution lines _ Initial sizing of installations and lines
Architect	Structural engineer	_ Site plan, building form, floor height _ Maximum and most common width of columns _ Rough specifications
Architect	Building services engineer	_ Site plan, building form and size _ Use, user numbers (e.g. number of employees if used as office) _ Building services requirements _ Floor plans

Tab.4:
Information typically required by the main planner in the design phase

From:	To:	Required information
Structural engineer	Architect	_ Main and secondary axes of loadbearing elements _ Preliminary dimensions
Building services engineer	Architect	_ Initial sizing of installations and lines _ Openings necessary for building services _ Cost estimate
Architect	Structural engineer	_ Dimensioned design development drawings (plans and sections), ready to be submitted for the building permit
Building services engineer	Structural engineer	_ Location of the main lines, location and loads of the installations
Architect	Building services engineer	_ Final design development drawings (plans, sections, views)
Structural engineer	Building services engineer	_ Design of loadbearing structure (girders, columns, loadbearing walls) _ Openings and slits in loadbearing elements

Tab.5:		
Information typically required by the main planner to prepare for construction		

From:	To:	Required information
Structural engineer	Architect	_ Formwork drawings _ Reinforcement drawings _ Connection details _ Bills of material
Building services engineer	Architect	_ Electrical, ventilation, heating, sanitary planning _ Drawings of wall openings and slits for building services _ Tendering documents, e.g. main lines for the invitation to tender for the building shell _ Defined responsibilities for other planning specialists
Architect	Structural engineer	_ Updated dimensioned plans and sections _ Working drawings, design details, specifications _ Specifications from the preliminary building notification or the building permit
Building services engineer	Structural engineer	_ Location of the main lines, location and loads of the installations _ Drawings of wall openings and slits
Architect	Building services engineer	_ Approved plans and perhaps specifications from the authorities _ Specifications _ Construction drawings
Structural engineer	Building services engineer	_ Formwork drawings, steel structure drawings and timber structure drawings _ Location of steel reinforcement for wall openings

UNIT PRODUCTION TIMES

Tab.6:
Sample unit production times to roughly estimate task durations

Work	UPT	Unit
Preparing the construction site		
Setting up crane	10-50	h/unit
Steel-lattice fence	0.2-0.4	h/m
Connecting utilities (electricity, water)	0.2-0.5	h/m
Excavation		
Excavating building pit	0.01-0.05	h/m^3
Excavating individual foundations with power shovel, including removal	0.05-0.3	h/m^3
Excavating individual foundations by hand	1.0-2.0	h/m^3
Concrete		
Rough estimate for complete building shell (700-1400 m^3 gross volume and 3-5 workers)	0.8-1.2	h/m^3 GV
Binding layer, unreinforced, d=5 cm	0.2	h/m^2
Bottom slab, reinforced cast-in-place concrete, d=20 cm	2.0	h/m^2
Ceiling, reinforced cast-in-place concrete, d=20 cm	1.6	h/m^2
Precast and partially precast concrete ceilings	0.4-0.9	h/m^2
Entire building, prefabricated	0.3-0.7	h/t
Casting concrete elements (without formwork or reinforcement)	0.4-0.5	h/m^3
Casting walls (without formwork and reinforcement)	1.0-1.5	h/m^3
Casting columns (without formwork and reinforcement)	1.5-2.0	h/m^3
Cast-in-place concrete stairway (without formwork and reinforcement)	3.0	h/unit
Large-panel formwork	0.6-1.0	h/m^2
Single formwork	1.0-2.0	h/m^2
Reinforcement	12-24	h/t

All types of sealing	0.25-0.40	h/m²
Scaffolding (assembly and disassembly)	0.1-0.3	h/m²
Masonry		
Loadbearing masonry wall	1.2-1.6	h/m³
Non-loadbearing interior wall	0.8-1.2	h/m³
Carpentry work		
Rafter roof, including joining and mounting (based on roof area)	0.5-0.7	h/m²
Roofing		
Flat roof (gravel), including complete mounting of non-insulated roof	0.5-0.7	h/m²
Pitched roof with roofing tiles	1.0-1.2	h/m²
Metal roofing	1.3-1.5	h/m²
Cladding for exterior walls		
Metal facade cladding	1.0-1.3	h/m²
Facing brick leaves	1.1-1.5	h/m³
Composite heat insulation system	0.6-0.8	h/m²
Assembly of precast concrete facades	0.5-0.7	h/m²
Exterior wall cladding with natural stone, slate, etc.	0.5-0.8	h/m²
Window construction		
Installing individual windows	1.5-2.5	h/unit
Installing roller shutter housing	0.6-1.5	h/unit
Roof windows	2.5-3.5	h/unit
Interior window sills	0.3-0.5	h/m
Plaster		
Exterior plastering	0.5-0.7	h/m²

Interior plastering, done by machine	0.2-0.4	h/m²
Interior plastering, manual	0.3-0.6	h/m²
Ceiling plaster	0.3-0.4	h/m²

Screed

Laying cement screed and anhydride screed (without membranes, insulation, etc.)	0.1-0.3	h/m²
Laying mastic asphalt screed (without membranes, insulation, etc.)	0.3-0.5	h/m²
Floating floor screed, including insulation layer	0.6-1.0	h/m²
Terrazzo screed, polished	2.0-2.5	h/m²

Dry construction

Drywall with plasterboard	0.2-0.5	h/m²
Prefabricated walls or wall paneling, single layer, including substructure	0.7-0.8	h/m²
Covering slanted ceilings	0.3-0.5	h/m²
Suspended ceiling structures	0.6-1.1	h/m²
Plasterboard stud wall, single panel	0.4-0.8	h/m²
Plasterboard stud wall, double panel	0.6-1.5	h/m²

Doors

Installing steel frames + door leaves	1.9-2.5	h/unit
Installing wooden doors	1.0-1.5	h/unit
Exterior doors	2.5-4.5	h/unit

Tiles, paving stones, cut stones

Floor tiling	0.5-1.8	h/m²
Wall tiling	1.3-2.5	h/m²
Natural and concrete paving stones	0.8-1.2	h/m
Baseboard made of tile or natural stone	0.3-0.4	h/m

Flooring

Creating level surface, filling holes	0.05-0.2	h/m²
PVC, linoleum and rolled flooring materials	0.3-0.6	h/m²
Needle felt or carpet on screed	0.1-0.4	h/m²
Baseboards	0.1-0.2	h/m²
Parquet floors, including surface treatment	1.2-1.8	h/m²
Sanding parquet floors, surface treatment	0.2-0.3	h/m²
Natural stone floors	0.9-1.2	h/m²
Stairway coverings	0.5-0.7	h/m²

Painting and wallpapering

Putty work	0.1-0.2	h/m²
Standard wallpaper (wall chip wallpaper, thick embossed wallpaper, etc.)	0.1-0.4	h/m²
Special wallpaper (velour, textile, wall images, etc.)	0.3-0.8	h/m²
Painting interior wall, single coat	0.05-0.2	h/m²
Painting interior wall, three coats	0.2-0.5	h/m²
Plastering and painting exterior wall	0.2-0.8	h/m²
Painting window, per coat	0.2-0.6	h/m²
Painting metal surface, all required coats (doors, sheet metal walls, etc.)	0.3-0.6	h/m²
Painting metal elements, all required coats (frames, sheet metal covering, etc.)	0.6-1.0	h/m²
Painting metal railings	0.1-0.3	h/m

Electrical work

Rough estimate for all electrical installations (700-1400 m³ gross volume and 2-3 workers)	0.2-0.4	h/m³ GV
Assembling cable tray + electrical lines	0.3-0.5	h/m
Assembling lights	0.3-0.8	h/unit

Assembling sub-distribution board	0.5-1.0	h/unit
Detailed installation of switches, outlets, etc.	0.02-0.05	h/unit

Heating, plumbing and sanitation installations

Rough estimate for complete heating installation (700-1400 m³ gross volume and 2-3 workers)	0.1-0.3	h/m³ GV
Rough estimate for complete gas, water and wastewater systems (700-1400 m³ gross volume and 2-3 workers)	0.15-0.4	h/m³ GV
Rough assembly of pipe routes	0.4-0.8	h/m
Rain and wastewater pipes	0.10-0.50	h/m
Detailed installation and assembly of sanitary fixtures	0.3-1.0	h/unit

THE AUTHOR

Bert Bielefeld holds a doctorate in engineering and works as a freelance architect in Dortmund. He is the managing director of the Aedis Pro-Manage project management company, teaches construction economics and construction management at the University of Siegen, and lectures at various architectural chambers and associations.

Series editor: Bert Bielefeld
Conception: Bert Bielefeld, Annette Gref
Layout and cover design: Muriel Comby
Translation into English: Adam Blauhut,
Joseph O'Donnell
English copy editing: Monica Buckland

All the photographs and figures in this book were
supplied by the author with the artistic assistance
of Irene Ens.

Library of Congress Control Number: 2008934152

Bibliographic information published by the German National Library
The German National Library lists this publication in the Deutsche Nationalbibliografie; detailed
bibliographic data are available on the Internet at
http://dnb.d-nb.de.

This book is also available in a German language
edition (ISBN 978-3-7643-8872-0).

© 2009 Birkhäuser Verlag AG
Basel · Boston · Berlin
P.O. Box 133, CH-4010 Basel, Switzerland
Part of Springer Science+Business Media

Printed on acid-free paper produced from
chlorine-free pulp. TCF ∞
Printed in Germany

ISBN 978-3-7643-8873-7
9 8 7 6 5 4 3 2 1   www.birkhauser.ch